Living to Impress Sucks

The Dangers of a Faked Life and How to Let Go of Your Constant Need for Approval

Living to Impress Sucks

Ralph Nyadzi

Published by Cegast Academy, 2024.

LIVING TO IMPRESS SUCKS

First edition. July 22, 2024.

ISBN: 979-8227096425

Written by Ralph Nyadzi.

Also by Ralph Nyadzi

Fast Track WASSCE General Arts
Fast Track WASSCE Government: Elements of Government

Standalone
Regrets
The Self-Support Guide
Becoming Self-Employed
Understanding Grammatical Names and Functions
Second Class Citizen Summary & Analysis
The Lion and the Jewel Summary & Analysis
WAEC Literature Poetry: Summary & Analysis
WAEC Literature African Poetry Summary & Analysis
WAEC Literature Non-African Poetry Summary & Analysis
What Makes A Hater
Living to Impress Sucks

Watch for more at https://www.cegastacademy.com.

Table of Contents

Introduction 1

PART 1: | UNDERSTANDING THE HABIT OF IMPRESSING OTHERS | Chapters 1 – 3 14

Chapter 1: The Trap of Living to Impress 15

Chapter 2: Identifying the Roots 20

Chapter 3: The Impact of Approval-Seeking on Personal Well-being 25

PART 2. RECOGNIZING YOUR FALSE IDENTITY | Chapters 4 and 5 33

Chapter 4: Self-Reflection and Awareness 34

Chapter 5: The Role of Social Media 38

PART 3: BREAKING FREE FROM THE HABIT | Chapters 6 to 8 42

Chapter 6: Building Authenticity 43

Chapter 7: Setting Boundaries in Your Daily Interactions 47

Chapter 8: Developing Healthy Relationships 51

PART 4: DISCOVERING INTENTIONAL LIVING Chapters 9 - 16 55

Chapter 9: The Meaning of Intentional Living 56

Chapter 10: Identifying Your True Values 61

Chapter 11: Setting Intentional Goals 66

Chapter 12: The Importance of Resisting Societal Pressures 72

Chapter 13: Choosing Authenticity in Relationships 78

Chapter 14: The Benefits of a Simplified Life...................................84

PART 5: SUSTAINING CHANGE Chapters 15 - 17......................90

Chapter 15: Finding Fulfilment in the Every Day 91

Chapter 16: Creating Lasting Habits 98

Chapter 17: 150 Living to Impress vs Intentional Living Quotes.... 102

Conclusion 115

To my mother, Fidelia... and my sisters: Kafui, Dzifa and Dzigbordi (Jay).

Introduction

A Story of Chasing Approval

Imagine living your life for the sole purpose of impressing others. Every decision you make, and every action you take, is driven by the need for approval and validation from those around you. This faked life could be your reality, regardless of whichever part of the world you are at this moment.

It was also the reality for Adam (Adam is not his real name), a 32-year-old banker from Lagos, Nigeria. Adam's life looked perfect from the outside: a high-paying job, a luxurious apartment, and a glamorous social life. However, beneath the surface, Adam was exhausted and deeply unhappy. His days were consumed by the pressure to maintain a facade, to be seen as successful and enviable by his peers.

One evening, after a particularly stressful day, Adam realized he was living a lie. He was constantly chasing the next big thing to impress others—buying expensive gadgets, attending exclusive parties, and posting meticulously curated photos on social media. But none of it brought him true happiness or fulfilment.

Adam's story is not unique; it mirrors the experiences of countless others who find themselves trapped in the cycle of living to impress.

The Difference Between Performance and Approval-Seeking

It's important to distinguish between situations where putting in a genuine effort to impress is appropriate and beneficial, and the unhealthy habit of living your entire life to gain approval from others.

Consider a job interview. In this competitive setting, it's perfectly normal and even expected to put your best foot forward. You prepare thoroughly, dress appropriately, and present your skills and achievements in the best possible light.

This effort is a positive and necessary part of demonstrating your qualifications and suitability for the job. It's a specific, short-term scenario where making a good impression serves a clear purpose and aligns with your genuine goals and values.

On the other hand, the unhelpful habit of living to impress others permeates every aspect of life. This behaviour goes beyond specific situations like job interviews and seeps into daily decisions and actions.

When your primary motivation for almost every decision you make is to gain approval from others or to receive benefits you don't truly deserve, it leads to a life of pretence.

You might find yourself buying things you can't afford, pretending to have interests you don't actually care about, or constantly comparing yourself and competing with others. This relentless pursuit of approval can cause stress, anxiety, and a sense of emptiness.

The key difference lies in intent and scope. Striving to impress in a job interview or similar competitive setting is about showcasing your true capabilities and putting in effort where it matters. Living to impress, however, is an ongoing, pervasive behaviour driven by a needless quest for external validation rather than internal fulfilment.

This book will help you recognize this difference and guide you toward a more intentional and authentic life.

Purpose of This Book

This book is a guide for anyone who desires to break free from the exhausting and unfulfilling habit of faking their life to impress others. It's also about adopting intentional living—a way of life that prioritizes your values, passions, and genuine connections over superficial approval.

Through this book, you will discover the transformative power of living authentically and intentionally.

In a world that constantly bombards us with images of perfection, it's easy to fall into the trap of living a life designed to impress others. Social media, peer pressure, and societal expectations often lead us to create a facade, hiding our true selves behind a mask of what we think others want to see. This book, *Living to Impress Sucks: The Dangers of a Faked Life and How to Let Go of Your Constant Need for Approval,* aims to help you break free from this exhausting cycle and discover the joy and fulfilment of living authentically.

We will explore the psychological roots of the need to impress, the consequences of maintaining a facade, and the incredible benefits of intentional living – a life lived by design and not by default.

Each chapter will offer practical advice, real-life examples, and exercises to help you transition from a life of impressing others to a life that truly reflects who you are.

A Friendly Self-Improvement Guide

This book is not about shaming anyone for their choices or past behaviours. Instead, it's a compassionate guide designed to help you understand why you might feel compelled to impress others. It doesn't stop there. The book goes a step further to provide you with practical steps to reclaim your true identity.

Whether you've just started to question your daily choices and the motives behind them or have been struggling with this issue for years, this book offers insights and tools to support your journey toward authenticity.

Does This Sound Like You?

Let me share a personal story I heard recently that inspired me to write this book. Listening to this story, made me remember my own life-changing personal story you will find out shortly. Hear this story directly from the narrator's own mouth:

A few years ago, I found myself trapped in a life that looked perfect from the outside. I had what looked like a successful career, a beautiful home, and a social media feed filled with enviable moments. But deep down, I was miserable. Every decision I made was driven by a need to impress others—my colleagues, my friends, even strangers on the internet.

One day, as I was scrolling through my carefully curated Instagram feed, I had an epiphany. I realized that the life I had been showing the world was a lie. It wasn't a reflection of my true self but a construct built to gain approval and admiration.

That moment of clarity set me on a path of self-discovery and transformation. I began peeling away the layers of my false identity so I could reconnect with who I really was. The journey wasn't easy, but it was the most rewarding experience of my life.

As I told you before, many people, including myself, have been there or are still struggling to set themselves free from the trap of living to impress others. We're like students of life - we may have made significant progress but we still have a long way to go.

Through this book, I want to share what I've learned with you. I want to help you avoid the pitfalls of living a faked life and guide you towards a more authentic, fulfilling existence.

My Personal Story: Conviction, Radicalism and Struggle

I've always felt that trying to impress others has never been my thing. And truly, in a lot of cases, this appears to be the case.

I once had to drop out of a class of youngsters studying and preparing for an annual ceremony in my church called 'Confirmation'. It looked to me like the whole exercise was meaningless and we were doing it just to win approval from our church leaders and parents.

On another occasion, I refused to wear a particular type of clothing for a church ceremony despite a distant aunt's insistence with support from my father. Here too, the reason they wanted me to wear that type of clothing was that everybody else in my group had one and wore one. It wasn't a uniform, though. I didn't have it. My parents couldn't afford it so they didn't have it.

The aunt who hysterically pressured me to wear one offered to give me one. But I wouldn't feel fine in borrowed clothes. Moreover, I was sure those relatives would later cast insinuations against my parents and siblings because of that 'kind' gesture.

So I stormed out angrily just before the event was billed to begin, went into my wooden hut room I helped my mother build barely a year before, locked myself inside and wouldn't respond to all the pleas coming from outside for me to come out, wear the borrowed cloth and participate in the event.

I didn't care about the fact that I was the lead performer in the said church ceremony. Those forcing me to conform and win empty approval should have known better - I told myself. The mere thought of appearing with a faked identity, in borrowed clothes just to impress everyone else was too offensive for my 14-year-old mind to take.

Look, I'm not proud that I disobeyed all those church leaders and elders including my father. But there was, and still is, something in me that refused to act just to please others at the expense of my personal comfort and values.

The most radical step I ever took to declare an all-out war on any tendency to impress others at my own expense was the day I said bye to my 9 to 5 job. I had just been working as a high school teacher for barely five months. That was my first posting after graduating from college with a degree in English.

One fateful morning, I told my colleague teachers I might never come back to school after that day. Let me be brief about my reasons. I was increasingly becoming unhappy with the job. I didn't like the work environment and I felt trapped. It was like I was pigeonholed, wasting my time and talents in that type of employment.

Moreover, I was scared I might end up being compelled to take or receive bribes or cut corners as the only means of survival. I simply hated such things (and I still do) but they were becoming so pervasive – like a national way of life.

I had dreams. I was ambitious. But I also valued integrity and entrepreneurship. Then I loved my freedom. I wanted to have full control over my time and financial destiny relying very much on the support and guidance of the Universe - the source of all creative energy and abundance.

My colleagues thought it was a joke but knew I was not good at making others laugh. I was more of an introverted and serious type. So concern showed on the faces of those who regarded themselves as my closest friends. But they still doubted it. Well, I did it. That was the last time I was in that school or any salaried job for that matter.

A few days later, some of my colleagues thought I had gone nuts. Others mocked me and told me in the face or behind my back I would come crawling back.

I vividly remember my headmaster and one other staff member coming to my newly established small grocery shop one day and angrily asking me to come back before he reported me to the authorities. I smiled to myself. He wouldn't understand. I never did.

Meanwhile, other people had their theories about my decision. While some put it down to the possibility that I failed my college final exams hence my sacking (laughable) by my employer, others were visibly confused.

I had gone against all that society expected of me: Go to school, excel academically if I can, get a good certificate, find a 'good' job, and leave a good impression on everyone else that matters.

It didn't matter if I found myself in a job that left me stranded financially halfway into every new month. That's fine and normal. And that's why it's normal too to find corrupt ways to appear to be doing well or at least minimize the number of your ever-present monthly creditors.

None of the above impressed me and I refused to impress others by remaining in a career I had found most unfulfilling. So I quit for good and I've been taking care of myself since. It hasn't been easy but I find my chosen path exciting and fulfilling.

Sometimes, throughout my life, I did horrible things just to resist the pressure to impress others and win their approval. Our world is indeed a sad and horrible place too. Too many people have this herd mindset. So many can't understand that it is possible to live contentedly without forcing to be someone else. And this is what ends up creating 'monsters' and widely misunderstood people like you and me.

I'm far from being perfect, after all.

But there are other times when I too make decisions that, upon a deeper reflection, get me thinking if I'm not guilty of the same bad habit of living to impress others.

The bottom line here is my situation is far from being perfect.

Here is a practical example.

Deep inside me, I feel that I'm more comfortable with a minimalist lifestyle. I don't want and need too many things for myself. I care very little about the grandiose comforts that others are constantly chasing. And, when I hear people emphasizing empty goals like making sure they have an expensive-looking living room, fleets of cars, a huge mansion for a residence and a wedding that would be the talk of the town, and to cap it all, a 'befitting burial' when the time comes or even for their loved ones, I cringe and smile sadly. These things mean nothing to me. Nothing at all.

But here is the thing. I'm the same person who has gone on to acquire things way beyond what I truly need. I'm consumed with what I consider an unhelpful passion for extras. Perhaps the psychology behind this mindset has got to do with my childhood history of lack and embarrassing financial inadequacy.

Today, even though, just like most normal human beings, I sometimes struggle financially, I'm always trying to build rooms that I hardly use for anything.

Yes, one motivation for this is indeed my desire to ensure those who will come after me, when I'm gone (without a 'befitting burial' costing an arm and a leg), will not suffer the same way my siblings, parents and I did decades ago.

While I'm convinced the things I do and the goals I pursue, are not meant for my personal comfort, I sometimes feel deep inside me, that I'm also doing so much just to spite or impress my detractors. I have a lot of them.

So am I not guilty of the same sin of living to impress others? I can live comfortably without most of the extras I keep acquiring. But isn't it selfish to think and behave as if the moment you're off the surface of this earth, everyone else will also disappear hence there's no need to work hard and leave a better life for generations after you?

Some selfish and manipulative preachers promote this dangerous mindset. They tell those who listen to them to stop chasing 'worldly' possessions. The porous logic is always this: *You will die anyway so why bother? Remember your end.*

I keep wondering if this line of thinking isn't nonsensical and disingenuous. Maybe you can help me answer these questions.

Here is one truth I know, though. Most of us are guilty of the unhelpful habit of trying hard to gain validation and approval from other people. The reasons for this are many and varied. And the consequences are never great for our well-being and desire to live happier and more fulfilling lives.

I've written this book to help anyone who genuinely sees the need to stop living a fake life just to impress and please others.

For My Own Benefit, Too

But here is my little confession. I needed to write this book for my benefit too. First, I want to properly organize my long-held personal thoughts and my findings about the subject. This move, I believe, will give me a huge sense of satisfaction.

Then I need this book to serve as a constant reminder for me personally each time I ought to rein in my constant urge to get unnecessary extras. And I want to read it frequently to assist me fight any tendency to make choices that serve no useful purpose but are only meant to impress or spite my numerous detractors.

As you can see, this book is as much for my guidance as it is for yours.

Are you in the category of those who wake up each day trying hard to avoid living a life of pretence without much success? Do you feel uncomfortable within your family, religious group, work environment, social club, friendship or marriage because you're being pressured to follow others who are busy living a culture of faked lives just to win approval or undeserved favours?

If you are tired of your faked life imposed on you by society or driven by personal greed and dishonesty, this book is for you. You will find at least some of the respite you seek from these pressures here.

Listen to me. It is possible to start being your true self, not worrying about what others think about you and not needing to act like a robot.

You will learn to be yourself. And that is what I believe is a life worth living.

Book Overview

Here's a brief overview of what you can expect in the chapters to come.

Part 1: Understanding the Habit of Impressing Others

This first part covers Chapters 1 to 3. We will explore the psychological and societal factors that drive us to seek external validation. You'll learn about the early influences, media pressures, and social dynamics that shape our behaviours.

Part 2: Recognizing Your False Identity

This part is divided into two chapters: 4 and 5. The segment focuses on self-reflection and awareness. You'll learn techniques to assess your behaviours and identify patterns that originate from a deep-seated need to impress others.

Part 3: Breaking Free from the Habit

Here, we'll dive into practical steps you can take to build authenticity, set boundaries, and develop healthy relationships. Real-life examples and exercises will help you apply these concepts to your own life. It covers Chapters 6 to 8.

Part 4: Discovering Intentional Living

Transitioning from a life driven by the need to impress to one of intentional living is not an overnight process. It requires self-reflection, commitment, and a willingness to change. However, the rewards are immense. By living intentionally, you will find greater peace, happiness, and fulfilment. You will build deeper and more meaningful relationships, and you will live a life that truly reflects who you are. These and more topics are what we will cover in Chapters 9 to 14.

Part 5: Sustaining Change

This final part covers Chapters 15 to 17.

It provides strategies for Sustaining change by finding fulfilment in the every day, creating lasting habits and staying motivated with transformational quotes about living to impress. You'll be inspired to maintain your new, authentic self and continue growing.

Conclusion

In the concluding segment, you will have a summary of the main points we've been discussing in the book. There are also helpful additional resources for further reading, practice and support.

What You Will Learn

Let's quickly go over the major benefits you're about to derive from reading this book.

Understanding the Trap of Living to Impress: You will start by identifying what it means to live for others' approval and why so many people fall into this trap.

The Consequences of Faking Your Life: You will also learn to appreciate the emotional, relational, and financial toll of constantly trying to impress.

Discovering Intentional Living: Thirdly, you'll learn about the principles of intentional living and how to use it to achieve a more fulfilling and authentic life.

Identifying Your True Values: Through exercises and examples, I'll help you identify your core values and align your actions with them.

Setting Intentional Goals: You'll learn how to set and achieve goals that reflect your true desires, not just societal expectations.

Overcoming Societal Pressures: Further, you'll acquire the skills needed to effectively resist external pressures and stay true to yourself.

Embracing Authenticity in Relationships: This book will help you appreciate the importance of honesty and vulnerability in building genuine connections.

Simplifying Your Life: Another significant benefit you'll gain from this book is that you can now declutter your whole life to focus on what truly matters.

Finding Fulfilment in the Everyday: You will learn how to find joy in simple pleasures and cultivate gratitude.

Creating a Sustainable Intentional Living Practice: Finally, you'll learn how to build and maintain habits that support intentional living.

Final Thoughts

As you set off on your path to a happier life that reflects your true self, remember that you are not alone. Many have walked this path before you and have found the courage to live authentically. This book is here to guide you every step of the way. So, take a deep breath, let go of the need to impress, and prepare to discover the incredible freedom and joy of living intentionally and on your own terms.

TIME FOR ACTION

Unlock the power of personal growth with our expert-guided courses. Start your journey to a better you today!

PART 1:

UNDERSTANDING THE HABIT OF IMPRESSING OTHERS

Chapters 1 – 3

Chapter 1: The Trap of Living to Impress

What Does It Mean to Live to Impress?

Living to impress others means constantly making decisions and acting based on the desire to gain approval, admiration, or validation from those around you. This behaviour often stems from a deep-seated need to be accepted and valued by others. People who live to impress typically prioritise how they are perceived over their true desires and values.

Common Signs and Behaviours

The first step towards changing this habit is to recognise the signs of living to impress other people. Here are some common behaviours to guide you.

1. Constant Need for Approval: You frequently look for validation from others to feel good about yourself.

2. Social Media Obsession: Your social media activity is heavily curated to present a perfect image. You often check likes, comments, and shares to gauge your worth.

3. Materialistic Pursuits: You buy and acquire things not because you need or truly want them, but because they will impress others.

4. Fear of Judgment: You avoid actions or decisions that might lead to criticism, even if they align with your true desires and values.

5. Comparing Yourself to Others: You constantly compare your life, achievements, and possessions to those of others, often feeling inadequate.

6. Inauthentic Behaviour: You adopt interests, hobbies, or opinions that don't resonate with you, just to fit in or be admired.

7. Backbiting and Finding Fault with Others: Direct personal attacks, indirect accusatory remarks and character assassination directed at a third party are tools you may be using to impress others.

Painting your innocent victims black has become your way of making yourself look good in the eyes of those you're desperately trying to impress. These victims of yours are usually people who, in your imagination, are a threat to you.

8. Rumour Mongering: You derive your false sense of validation from appearing to be knowledgeable by spreading falsehoods and half-truths about people and events.

The people at the receiving end of your unhelpful behaviour are mostly individuals whose life stories you hardly know anything about.

Historical Perspective on Impressing Others

From ancient civilizations to modern society, the desire to impress others has been a constant part of the human experience. In ancient Rome, people displayed their wealth and status through grand architecture and lavish parties.

In the Victorian era, social status was often showcased through elaborate etiquette and fashionable attire. This need to project a certain image is deeply rooted in our social history and evolved alongside human society.

Today, the platforms have changed, but the underlying drivers remain the same. Social media profiles, luxury cars, designer clothes, and the latest gadgets are modern symbols of success and status.

Understanding the historical context of this behaviour helps us see that it's not a new phenomenon but an ingrained part of our collective psyche.

Psychological Factors

At its core, the habit of trying to gain approval from others stems from fundamental psychological needs. Psychologists identify several key factors that drive this behaviour.

1. Need for Acceptance: Humans are inherently social creatures. From an early age, we seek acceptance from our peers, family, and society.

This need for belonging can lead us to adopt behaviours and attitudes that we believe will make us more acceptable to others.

2. Self-Esteem and Self-Worth: Our self-esteem is often influenced by how others perceive us. When we receive positive feedback and admiration, it boosts our self-worth. Conversely, criticism and rejection can damage our self-esteem, driving us to seek further validation.

3. Fear of Rejection: The fear of being rejected or ostracized can be a powerful motivator. To avoid this, we may conform to societal expectations and present ourselves in ways that we believe will be more appealing to others – often to the detriment of our personal values and ideals.

4. Comparison and Competition: Social comparison theory suggests that we determine our own social and personal worth based on how we stack up against others. This can lead to a constant cycle of comparison and competition, pushing us to impress others to feel superior or at least equal.

Case Studies

To illustrate these psychological factors, let's look at some real-life examples:

Godwin's Career: Godwin, a successful lawyer, constantly felt the need to work long hours and take on high-profile cases to gain the admiration of his peers and superiors. Despite his success, he felt empty and unfulfilled, always chasing the next achievement to validate his worth.

Becky's Social Media Life: Becky, a social media influencer, spent hours curating the perfect posts and maintaining an image of a glamorous lifestyle. Behind the scenes, she was struggling with anxiety and depression, driven by the pressure to keep up appearances and impress her followers.

Kumalo's Social Circle: Kumalo, a young professional, surrounded himself with people who valued material success. He bought expensive clothes, cars, and gadgets to fit in, even though he was accumulating debt. His fear of rejection kept him trapped in this cycle of impressing others at the expense of his financial well-being.

These examples highlight how deeply the need to impress others can impact our lives, often leading to negative consequences. Your awareness of these psychological drivers is the first step toward breaking free from the habit.

Conclusion

In this chapter, we've explored the meaning of living to impress others, behaviours that demonstrate this attitude, the historical context and psychological factors that contribute to the habit of trying to impress others. Our recognition of these influences will enable us to understand why we behave this way and how it affects our well-being.

In the next chapter, we will take a much closer look at the roots of this behaviour. We shall examine the early influences and societal pressures that shape our desire for external validation.

TIME FOR ACTION

Unlock the power of personal growth with our expert-guided courses. Start your journey to a better you today!

Chapter 2: Identifying the Roots

Early Influences

Our early experiences from childhood profoundly shape our behaviours and attitudes. The desire to impress others often begins in childhood, influenced by various factors. Let's examine some of these factors.

1. Upbringing and Family Dynamics: Childhood experiences and family expectations can shape your desire for approval. If you grew up in an environment where love and acceptance were conditional, you might end up developing a habit of seeking validation.

2. Parental Expectations: Many parents have high hopes and expectations for their children. While this can be positive, it can also lead to a child feeling pressured to live up to these expectations. Children learn early on to seek approval from their parents, and this can translate into a lifelong habit of seeking validation from others.

3. School Environment: The school environment is a microcosm of society, where children learn social norms and hierarchies. Academic performance, athletic achievements, and social status can all become measures of worth. The desire to impress teachers, peers, and even parents can drive children to adopt behaviours that win approval.

4. Sibling Rivalry: Parents and older relatives often draw unnecessary comparisons between siblings. This can start in children a competitive spirit, where they feel the need to outperform one another to gain recognition and approval from critical family members.

5. Cultural and Societal Norms: Cultural and societal norms also play a significant role. In some cultures, honour and reputation are paramount. Thus, individuals may feel an intense pressure to conform to these standards to maintain family or community honour.

Media and Pop Culture

The media and pop culture significantly influence our perceptions of success and happiness. From a young age, we are bombarded with images and messages that shape our understanding of what it means to be successful and happy.

Here are some examples.

1. **Television and Movies:** Characters in television shows and movies often lead glamorous lives filled with wealth, beauty, and adventure. These portrayals can create unrealistic expectations and pressure to emulate these lifestyles.

2. **Advertising:** Advertisements often play on our insecurities. Most adverts tend to suggest that buying certain products will make us more attractive, successful, or happy. This constant exposure can lead us to believe that our worth is tied to the things we own and the image we project.

3. **Social Media:** Social media platforms have intensified the pressure to impress others. The curated and often exaggerated lives we see on social media can make us feel inadequate. They push us to present an equally impressive image to keep up with our peers.

Peer Pressure and Social Dynamics

The need to belong and be accepted by our peers is a powerful force that shapes human behaviour.

1. **Friendship Circles:** Within our friendship circles, there is often an unspoken expectation to conform to certain behaviours, interests, and

lifestyles. The desire to fit in and be liked can lead us to adopt these behaviours, even if they don't align with our true selves.

2. Workplace Culture: In the workplace, the pressure to impress colleagues and superiors can be intense. Professional success and social acceptance often go hand in hand, leading us to prioritize our image and achievements over our well-being.

3. Community and Social Groups: Our community and social groups can also exert pressure on us to conform to certain standards. Whether it's through religious institutions, social clubs, or community organizations, the desire to be seen as a valuable member of the group can drive us to adopt behaviours that seek to win approval.

4. Societal Pressures: Society often places high value on wealth, status, and appearance. This pressure can make you feel compelled to live up to these standards, even if they don't align with your true self.

Case Studies

To better understand these influences, let's look at some real-life examples.

Alicia's Upbringing: Alicia grew up in a household where academic excellence was highly valued. Her parents constantly compared her achievements to those of her older siblings. As a result, Alicia felt intense pressure to excel in her studies to gain her parents' approval. This habit of seeking validation through achievements followed her into adulthood. It affected her career choices and personal relationships.

Uche's Media Consumption: Uche spent his teenage years consuming media that portrayed wealth and luxury as the ultimate goals. He became obsessed with the idea of owning expensive cars and living a lavish lifestyle. This obsession led him to make financial decisions that were more about impressing others than meeting his own needs.

Dzifa's Social Circle: Dzifa's friends were all high achievers who constantly shared their successes on social media. Feeling the pressure to keep up, Dzifa started fabricating stories about her own achievements. This behaviour created a cycle of deceit that strained her friendships and affected her self-esteem.

These examples highlight how early influences, media, and peer pressure can shape our attitudes and drive us to seek external validation. You must, therefore appreciate these fundamental causes to fully understand the universal habit of trying to impress others. Indeed, it is the first step towards breaking free from it.

Marcia's Story

Marcia, a 28-year-old graphic designer from Brazil, spent years living to impress others. She meticulously curated her social media profiles, always sharing photos of exotic vacations, trendy restaurants, and stylish outfits. Her friends admired her glamorous lifestyle, but behind the scenes, Marcia was struggling. She was deeply in debt, constantly anxious, and felt disconnected from her true self.

Marcia's turning point came when she attended a high school reunion. She realized she had lost touch with who she really was. The person she presented to the world was a fabrication, crafted to gain admiration and approval. This realization led Marcia to embark on a journey of self-discovery and intentional living. She started by taking a break from social media, focusing on her true passions, and reconnecting with old friends who knew her authentic self. Today, Marcia feels more at peace and content, no longer burdened by the need to impress others.

Conclusion

In this chapter, we've explored the various factors that contribute to the habit of impressing others, from early influences and media to peer pressure and social dynamics. By identifying these roots, we can begin to understand why we behave the way we do and start to take steps towards changing these patterns.

In the next chapter, we will look into the impact that living to impress others has on our well-being including its long-term effects on our mental health, relationships, and career life.

TIME FOR ACTION

Unlock the power of personal growth with our expert-guided courses. Start your journey to a better you today!

Chapter 3: The Impact of Approval-Seeking on Personal Well-being

The effects of the habit of living just for the sake of impressing others or seeking approval from others can, in many ways, undermine one's quest for personal growth.

Here now come the major consequences of faking your life. I trust that they will give you enough motivation to take the necessary steps that will allow you to let go of a habit that is, for all intents and purposes, a trap.

Emotional Toll and Mental Health Issues

Faking your life to impress others takes a significant emotional toll. Constantly maintaining a facade requires immense mental energy and can lead to various negative emotional outcomes

Also, living to impress others can have profound effects on your mental health. Thus, the constant need to seek external validation can lead to various emotional and mental health issues including the following.

1. Stress and Anxiety: Trying to keep up appearances or live up to others' expectations can be incredibly stressful. The fear of being exposed as a fraud will keep you in a constant state of dread.

Further, the pressure to maintain a facade and meet others' expectations can cause chronic anxiety. This anxiety stems from the fear of not being good enough and the constant worry about how others perceive you.

2. Depression: When your self-worth is tied to how much external approval you get, it can result in feelings of inadequacy and hopelessness especially when you're unable to meet these standards.

This can lead to depression, as you feel trapped in a cycle of seeking validation and feeling unfulfilled. Over time, the disconnect between your true self and the persona you present can lead to feelings of emptiness. The lack of genuine fulfilment and the constant pressure to impress can be overwhelming.

3. Low Self-Esteem: Relying on others for validation can erode your self-esteem. Instead of feeling confident in your own worth, you become dependent on the opinions of others. So, any perceived failure to impress can lead to feelings of inadequacy and self-doubt. This quickly develops in you a fragile sense of self-worth that can easily be shattered by any negative criticism or rejection.

4. Perfectionism: Your unending drive to impress others often leads to perfectionism. This unrealistic standard sets you up for failure and disappointment, as you strive for an unattainable ideal. It makes you perpetually dissatisfied with yourself. This may relate to your physical appearance, your circle of friends, material possessions, your academic performance, career choice and relationship choices.

Physical Health Impact

The stress and anxiety associated with living to impress others can also take a toll on your physical health.

1. Sleep Problems: Stress and anxiety can lead to sleep disturbances, including insomnia. Lack of sleep can affect your overall health, mood, and productivity.

2. Chronic Illness: Prolonged stress can weaken your immune system, making you more susceptible to illnesses. Conditions like hypertension, heart disease, and other stress-related illnesses can develop over time. The sad part is you may never suspect your approval-seeking behaviour as the cause of your chronic health problems.

3. Unhealthy Coping Mechanisms: To manage stress, you might turn to unhealthy coping mechanisms such as overeating, smoking, or excessive alcohol consumption, all of which worsen your physical health issues.

Relationship Strains

Living to impress not only affects your mental health but also strains your relationships. Authentic connections are built on honesty and vulnerability, but when you're focused on impressing others, these essential elements can be compromised.

This may be the reason why your relationships are significantly impacted. The authenticity and depth of your connections may be suffering because you prioritize image over genuine connections.

1. Superficial Relationships: When you focus on impressing others, your relationships can become shallow. Instead of building deep, meaningful connections, you create relationships based on appearances and status. Such relationships lack true emotional intimacy leaving you feeling dissatisfied and empty. People may like you for your facade, not for who you truly are, leading to superficial connections that lack depth and meaning.

2. Trust Issues: Living a facade can lead to trust issues. If people discover that you're not being genuine, it can create suspicion, erode trust and damage your relationships with long-term consequences. Conversely, you may also struggle to trust others, fearing that they, too, are not being authentic.

3. Conflict and Resentment: The pressure to impress can lead to conflicts in relationships. You may feel resentful towards those you're desperately trying to impress with little success, while they, realizing your self-serving intentions, may feel frustrated by your inauthentic behaviour. This can create a cycle of misunderstanding and tension.

4. Co-dependency: The need for external validation can result in co-dependent relationships. You easily become reliant on others for your sense of self-worth. Without them, you're nothing, so to speak. The resulting unhealthy dynamics mean that your self-esteem, happiness and pride in your identity are forever linked to what other people think or say about you.

5. Isolation: As you prioritize impressing others, you may neglect genuine relationships with those who love and accept you for who you are. This can lead to feelings of isolation and loneliness.

Career or Professional Life

In the workplace or business environment, the habit of trying to impress others can affect our career satisfaction and growth.

1. Burnout: The constant drive to achieve and impress can lead to burnout. The more you push yourself beyond your limits to gain approval, the greater your risks of physical and emotional exhaustion. And, as you may know, this can negatively impact your productivity and overall well-being.

2. Low Sense of Fulfilment: Some people choose certain careers based on what impresses others rather than what truly interests them. This can lead to a lack of fulfilment. Are you one of such? You may find yourself in jobs or business fields that don't align with your true passions and values. This will leave you feeling unfulfilled and disconnected from our work. Underachievement or complete failure are possible long-term outcomes.

3. Workplace Relationships: Your frantic attempts to unnecessarily impress colleagues and superiors can strain your workplace relationships. It can create a competitive and distrustful environment, where collaboration and genuine connections are undermined by the pressure to outperform and outshine others.

4. Inauthentic and Poor Leadership: For those in leadership positions, the need to impress can result in inauthentic leadership. Leaders who prioritize image over integrity may struggle to build trust and respect within their team. Ultimately, this attitude destroys their effectiveness and the team's success.

Financial Burden

Trying to keep up appearances often comes with a financial cost. Whether it's buying the latest gadgets, wearing trendy clothes, or dining at expensive restaurants, the need to impress can lead to significant financial strain.

1. Debt Accumulation: Many people fall into debt trying to maintain a lifestyle they can't afford. Credit cards and loans might provide a temporary solution, but they can lead to long-term financial problems.

2. Financial Stress: The pressure to spend money to impress others can cause significant financial stress. Worrying about how to pay bills or manage debt can add to the emotional toll of living to impress.

3. Sacrificing Needs for Wants: In your quest to impress, you will end up sacrificing essential needs for non-essential wants. This can lead to financial instability and compromise your long-term financial health.

Case Studies

Let's take a quick look at some real-life examples to illustrate these effects of the habit of living to impress others.

Agatha's Anxiety: Agatha, a marketing executive, constantly felt the need to prove herself to her boss and colleagues. The pressure to exceed expectations led to chronic anxiety. It affected her ability to concentrate and perform well at work. Despite her achievements, she never felt good enough and was always on edge.

Ken's Relationships: Ken, a socialite, built his relationships on appearances. He always presented a polished image, hiding his true self from his friends. Over time, Ken realized that his friendships lacked depth and genuine connection. When his facade began to crumble, he found it difficult to trust others and began to feel isolated.

Halima's Career: Halima pursued a high-paying corporate job to impress her family and peers. Despite her success, she felt unfulfilled and disconnected from her work. The constant need to maintain her image led to burnout, and she eventually decided to leave her job to pursue a career that aligned with her true passions.

Personal Story: Arthur's Struggle

Arthur, a 35-year-old software developer from Australia, spent years trying to impress his colleagues and friends. He drove an expensive car, wore designer clothes, and hosted lavish parties.

On social media, Arthur's life appeared perfect. However, behind the scenes, he was struggling. The financial strain of maintaining his faked lifestyle led to mounting debt, and the pressure to keep up appearances caused significant stress and anxiety.

Arthur's breaking point came when he realized he couldn't afford his mortgage payments. The risk of becoming homeless started him in the face. The facade he had worked so hard to maintain was crumbling, and he felt overwhelmed by the fear of being exposed.

This crisis forced Arthur to re-evaluate his priorities and make drastic changes. He sold his expensive car, downsized his home, and started focusing on his true passions and values.

Today, Arthur lives a simpler, more intentional life. He has built genuine relationships and found peace in being his authentic self.

These examples, including Arthur's sobering personal story, highlight the fact that faking your life to impress others can have serious emotional, relational, financial, and physical consequences.

Recognizing these consequences is crucial in motivating you to make changes and embrace a more authentic and intentional life. By breaking free from the cycle of impressing others, you can find true fulfilment, build meaningful relationships, and live a life that genuinely reflects who you are.

Illustration: The Vicious Cycle of Impressing Others

To better understand the consequences of living to impress, consider the following illustration of the cycle.

1. Desire for Approval: The cycle begins with the desire for approval and validation from others.

2. Inauthentic Behaviour: To gain approval, you engage in behaviours that are not a true reflection of who you are.

3. Temporary Satisfaction: Approval from others provides temporary satisfaction, and thus reinforces the behaviour.

4. Increased Pressure: The need to maintain the façade to avoid detection and seek further approval grows, leading to increased pressure and stress.

5. Negative Consequences: Emotional, relational, financial, and physical consequences arise.

6. Cycle Repeats: The negative consequences lead to a deeper desire for approval, thereby perpetuating the cycle.

Conclusion

In this chapter, we've identified the various ways that living to impress others can impact our personal well-being. From mental health issues and strained relationships to career dissatisfaction and burnout, the consequences are far-reaching and profound. Understanding these impacts helps us see the importance of addressing this habit and taking steps towards a more authentic life.

In the next chapter, we will focus on recognizing your false identity. We'll explore how techniques for self-reflection and awareness, can help you identify patterns of behaviour aimed at impressing others.

TIME FOR ACTION

Unlock the power of personal growth with our expert-guided courses. Start your journey to a better you today!

PART 2. RECOGNIZING YOUR FALSE IDENTITY
Chapters 4 and 5

Chapter 4: Self-Reflection and Awareness

The road to breaking free from the habit of living to impress others begins with self-reflection and awareness. Here are some effective techniques to help you assess your behaviours and uncover your true self.

Techniques for Self-Assessment

1. Journaling: Writing about your life in a journal is a powerful way to explore your thoughts and feelings and understand your actions and motivations. Set aside time each day to write about your experiences. Focus on situations where you felt the need to impress others or acted in ways that betrayed a deep-seated need to impress people. Ask yourself why you behaved a certain way and what you were hoping to achieve. Over time, patterns will begin to emerge that can help you understand your motivations.

2. Mindfulness Meditation: Mindfulness meditation helps you stay present and become more aware of your thoughts and feelings. By practising mindfulness, you can develop a deeper understanding of your triggers and responses. Start with a few minutes of meditation each day, gradually increasing the time as you become more comfortable with the practice.

3. Self-Questioning: Ask yourself probing questions to gain insight into your behaviour. Some questions to consider include:

- Why do I feel the need to impress others?

- What am I hoping to achieve by seeking external validation?

- How do I feel when I don't receive the approval I'm seeking?

- What aspects of my life are influenced by the need to impress others?

- How would I behave if I didn't care about others' opinions?

4. Feedback from Trusted Friends: Sometimes, it can be difficult to see our behaviours. Ask trusted friends or family members for their observations. They can provide valuable insights into how you present yourself and when you might be trying to impress others. Be open to their feedback and use it as a tool for self-improvement.

Identifying Patterns of Behaviour

Once you've started your self-assessment, the next step is to recognize patterns in your daily behaviour. Look for recurring themes and situations where you feel compelled to impress others. Here are some common patterns to watch for.

1. Social Media Behaviour: Pay attention to how you use social media. Do you post things primarily to receive likes and positive comments? Do you feel disappointed or anxious when your posts don't get the reaction you hoped for? Your awareness of these patterns can help you understand the role social media plays in your need for validation.

2. Conversations and Interactions: Pay close attention to how you interact with others. Do you frequently talk about your achievements or possessions? Do you exaggerate or embellish stories to make yourself seem more impressive? Your ability to identify these behaviours can help you see when you're seeking approval.

3. Decision-Making: Reflect on how you make decisions. Are your choices influenced by what others will think? Do you prioritize appearances over your happiness and well-being? When you understand these patterns it can help you make more authentic decisions, going forward.

4. Emotional Responses: Pay attention to your emotional responses. Do you feel anxious, stressed, or unhappy when you don't receive the validation you seek? Do you experience a temporary boost in self-esteem when you do? Recognizing these emotional patterns can help you break the cycle of seeking external validation.

Case Studies

Let's look at some examples of individuals who have successfully recognized and confronted their false identities.

Rachel's Social Media Detox: Rachel realized that her obsession with social media was driven by a need for external validation. She decided to take a break from social media for a month, using that time to reflect on her true interests and passions. During her detox, she discovered a love for painting and began sharing her art with a small, supportive group of friends instead of seeking approval from a broader audience.

David's Career Shift: David was a successful investment banker, but he felt unfulfilled and stressed. After some deep self-reflection, he realized that his career choice was influenced by a desire to impress his family and friends. David decided to pursue his true passion for teaching, eventually becoming a high school math teacher. While the career change was challenging, he found immense satisfaction and fulfilment in his new role.

Joy's Authentic Conversations: Joy noticed that she often bragged about her achievements in conversations with friends and colleagues. She began practising mindfulness and journaling, which helped her become more aware of her behaviour. Joy made a conscious effort to have more authentic conversations, focusing on genuine connection rather than impressing others. As a result, her relationships deepened, and she felt more confident in her true self.

These examples demonstrate the power of self-reflection and awareness in recognizing and confronting false identities. By using these techniques, you can gain a deeper understanding of your behaviour and start making changes towards a more authentic life.

Conclusion

In this chapter, we've discovered the importance of self-reflection and awareness in breaking free from the habit of impressing others. By using techniques like journaling, mindfulness meditation, self-questioning, and seeking feedback, you can gain valuable insights into your behaviour and recognize patterns that drive your need for external validation. The next step is to use this awareness to start building a more authentic life.

We will begin this stage by acknowledging the significant role social media plays in creating and maintaining fake lives in our current age and time. You will uncover effective strategies for moderating your social media use and come up close with real-life examples of individuals who have successfully overcome this challenge.

TIME FOR ACTION

Unlock the power of personal growth with our expert-guided courses. Start your journey to a better you today!

Chapter 5: The Role of Social Media

The Illusion of Perfection

Social media platforms like Facebook, WhatsApp, Instagram, and Twitter have transformed how we connect with others and present ourselves to the world. While these platforms offer numerous benefits, they also perpetuate the illusion of perfection, which can fuel your need to impress others. Here are some ways social media contributes to this issue:

1. Curated Lives: Social media allows us to curate the best parts of our lives, creating a highlight reel that often doesn't reflect reality. This curated content can make it seem like everyone else except you is living a perfect life. This false realization instantly makes you feel inadequate and pushes you to project an equally impressive image.

2. Comparison Culture: The constant exposure to others' seemingly perfect lives fosters a culture of comparison. We compare our behind-the-scenes with others' highlight reels. Such unrealistic comparisons can lead to feelings of envy, jealousy, inadequacy, and dissatisfaction with our own lives.

3. Validation through Likes, Comments and Shares: Social media platforms are designed to reward us with likes, comments, and shares. These forms of validation can become addictive. They make us constantly seek approval from our online audience. This need for validation can drive you to post content that impresses others rather than reflects your true self.

4. Filters and Editing: Today, the widespread use of filters and photo-editing apps allows us to artificially enhance our appearances. We thus create and post images and videos that may not be realistic or normal. This has contributed to the craze to achieve unrealistic beauty standards that only further the illusion of perfection.

Detox and Moderation

The first step is your appreciation of the significant role social media plays in perpetuating the unrelenting quest to impress others. The next step is to take practical measures to moderate its use and reduce its influence. Here are some strategies you can personally implement to help you detox and find a healthier balance.

1. Digital Detox: Take a break from social media for a set period, say a day, a week, or a month. Use this time to focus on offline activities that bring you joy and fulfilment. Reflect on how the detox affects your mood and self-esteem.

2. Set Boundaries: Establish clear boundaries for your social media use. Limit the amount of time you spend on these platforms each day and avoid using them during certain times, such as before bed or during meals. Use apps or built-in features on your phone to track and manage your screen time.

3. Declutter Your Feed: Be intentional about who you follow and what content you consume. Unfollow or mute accounts that make you feel inadequate or that perpetuate unrealistic standards. Instead, follow accounts that inspire, educate, and uplift you.

4. Mindful Posting: Before posting on social media, ask yourself why you're sharing the content. Is it to seek validation or to share something meaningful? Aim to post content that reflects your true self and values rather than what you think will impress others.

5. Engage Authentically: Use social media to build genuine connections rather than to seek validation. Engage with others in meaningful ways, such as leaving thoughtful comments or sharing supportive messages. Focus on the quality of your interactions rather than the quantity of likes and followers.

Real-Life Examples

To illustrate these strategies, let's look at some real-life examples of individuals who have successfully moderated their social media use.

Mariama's Digital Detox: Mariama realized that she was spending hours each day scrolling through social media, leaving her feeling anxious and inadequate. She decided to take a month-long digital break. During this time, she focused on her hobbies, spent time with loved ones, and practised mindfulness. By the end of the month, Mariama felt more present and content. She decided to limit her social media use to 30 minutes a day and noticed a significant improvement in her mental well-being.

Alonso's Mindful Posting: Alonso, a photographer, used to post daily on Instagram, constantly seeking validation from his followers. He noticed that this need for approval was affecting his creativity and self-esteem. Alonso started to practice mindful posting, sharing only his most meaningful work and including captions that reflected his true thoughts and experiences. He also began engaging more authentically with his followers, responding to comments and sharing insights about his creative process. This shift allowed Alonso to build deeper connections with his audience. Now, he felt more fulfilled in his work.

Sophia's Decluttered Feed: Sophia followed many influencers and celebrities on social media, often comparing herself to their seemingly perfect lives. She decided to curate her feed, unfollowing accounts that made her feel inadequate and following accounts that promoted body positivity, mental health awareness, and personal growth. This change helped Sophia shift her focus from comparison to self-acceptance. It inspired her to live a more authentic life.

These examples clearly show how moderating social media use and adopting healthier habits can help reduce the pressure to impress others and promote a more authentic lifestyle.

Conclusion

In this chapter, we've discussed the role of social media in creating and maintaining false identities. The illusion of perfection and the culture of comparison can significantly impact our self-esteem and drive us to seek external validation.

Here is the lesson: A simple decision to implement the above strategies like digital detoxes, setting boundaries, curating your feeds, and engaging mindfully, will help you reduce the influence of social media. Ultimately, you will be on the way to building a more authentic version of yourself.

In the next chapter, we will discuss building authenticity. We'll explore the importance of embracing your true self, provide practical exercises to help you discover and nurture your authenticity, and share success stories of individuals who have built authentic lives.

TIME FOR ACTION

Unlock the power of personal growth with our expert-guided courses. Start your journey to a better you today!

PART 3: BREAKING FREE FROM THE HABIT

Chapters 6 to 8

Chapter 6: Building Authenticity

Embrace Your True Self

Accepting your true self is a transformative process that involves shedding the layers of pretence and stepping into your genuine identity. It requires self-compassion, courage, and a commitment to living in alignment with your values and desires. Here are some key steps to help you embrace your true self.

1. Self-Acceptance: Begin by accepting yourself as you are, with all your strengths and weaknesses. Recognize that no one is perfect, and it's okay to have flaws and make mistakes. Self-acceptance is the foundation of building an authentic, confident life that needs no external approval.

2. Identify Your Values: Take time to reflect on your core values. What matters most to you? What principles guide your decisions and actions? Knowing your values helps you make choices that align with your true self.

3. Listen to Your Inner Voice: Pay attention to your intuition and inner voice. Often, we ignore our gut feelings in favour of external opinions. Trusting yourself and following your intuition will help you resist the temptation to build a faked life whose primary goal is to please others.

4. Let Go of Approval-Seeking: Release the need to seek approval from others. Understand that you cannot please everyone, and that's okay. Focus on living in a way that feels true to you, regardless of others' opinions.

5. Practice Self-Compassion: Be kind to yourself. Treat yourself with the same love and understanding that you would offer a close friend.

Self-compassion helps you navigate challenges and setbacks without harsh self-judgment.

Practical Exercises

Here are some practical exercises to help you discover and nurture your authenticity.

1. Values Clarification Exercise:

- Write down a list of values that resonate with you (e.g., peace, honesty, compassion, creativity).

- Narrow the list down to your top five core values.

- Reflect on how these values manifest in your daily life and decisions. Are there areas where you could align more closely with your values?

2. Inner Child Meditation:

- Find a quiet place and close your eyes.

- Visualize yourself as a child. What did you love to do? What were your dreams and passions?

- Imagine hugging your inner child and telling them that it's okay to be themselves.

- Reflect on how you can incorporate those childhood passions and dreams into your current life.

3. Authentic Action List:

- Make a list of actions that reflect your true self. These could be small, everyday actions or larger life changes.

- Commit to incorporating at least one authentic action into your daily routine.

- Track your progress and reflect on how these actions make you feel.

4. Self-Reflection Journaling:

- Set aside time each day to journal about your experiences, thoughts, and feelings.

- Ask yourself questions like, "What did I do today that felt authentic?" and "Were there moments when I acted out of a desire to impress others?"

- Use your journal to explore your authentic self and identify areas for growth.

Case Studies

It's time to look at some success stories of individuals who have embraced their true selves and built authentic lives.

Brenda's Career Change: Brenda worked in a high-stress corporate job that left her feeling unfulfilled. After reflecting on her values and passions, she realized that her true calling was in the creative arts. Despite the fear of judgment from her peers, Brenda left her job and pursued a career as a graphic designer. She now feels more aligned with her true self and finds joy in her work.

Carlos's Authentic Relationships: Carlos noticed that many of his friendships were based on impressing others and superficial interactions. He decided to focus on building deeper, more meaningful relationships. Carlos started being more open and vulnerable with his friends. He freely shared his true thoughts and feelings. As a result, his relationships became more trusting, fulfilling and supportive.

Lena's Self-Expression: Lena had always loved fashion but felt pressured to conform to societal expectations. She decided to embrace her unique sense of style and started dressing in a way that reflected her true personality. Lena's confidence grew as she expressed herself authentically, and she inspired others to do the same.

These real-life examples underscore the transformative power of embracing your true self. By aligning with your values, trusting your intuition, and letting go of approval-seeking, you can build a life that reflects your authentic identity.

Conclusion

In this chapter, we've explored the importance of building authenticity. We identified practical exercises that can help you embrace your true self. Remember that embracing authenticity involves self-acceptance, identifying your values, listening to your inner voice, and practising self-compassion. By taking these steps, you can create a more fulfilling and genuine life.

In the next chapter, we will discuss the importance of setting boundaries. We'll explore why boundaries are crucial for maintaining authenticity, provide practical steps for setting and maintaining boundaries, and share real-life scenarios where setting boundaries led to positive changes.

TIME FOR ACTION

Unlock the power of personal growth with our expert-guided courses. Start your journey to a better you today!

Chapter 7: Setting Boundaries in Your Daily Interactions

The Importance of Boundaries

Boldly setting your boundaries and being uncompromising about them are crucial aspects of maintaining authenticity and protecting your well-being. Your personal boundaries define the limits of other people's behaviours you're willing to accommodate. Such red lines help you preserve your energy, self-respect, and mental health. Here's why personal boundaries are essential in our dealings with others.

1. Protecting Your Well-being: Boundaries help you safeguard your mental and emotional health by preventing others from overstepping and causing you stress or discomfort.

2. Maintaining Authenticity: Clear boundaries allow you to stay true to yourself by defining what is acceptable and what is not. This helps you avoid compromising your values and priorities to please others. With such boundaries, you will hardly be forced to fake your life and suffer privately under the burdens a faked life imposes on you.

3. Building Respectful Relationships: Boundaries promote mutual respect in relationships. When you set clear limits, others learn to respect your needs and preferences, leading to healthier and more balanced interactions.

4. Preventing Burnout: By setting limits on your time and energy, boundaries help you avoid detractions, overcommitment and burnout. Your red lines enable you to focus on what truly matters to you.

5. Protecting Your Resources: You will be able to preserve the resources that matter most to you such as time, money, buildings and other belongings only if the people you come into contact with know the extent to which they are allowed to go in using and depleting what you've worked hard to build.

6. Discouraging Undue Advantage Takers: Without clear red lines, trust others to take undue advantage of your excessive kindness and tolerance. Boundaries help you remain in control of your life so you're not forced to please others to your discomfort.

How to Set Boundaries

Now that you know why you must boldly draw red lines or boundaries so others don't force you to be a faked version of yourself or take undue advantage of you, it's time to learn how to set your boundaries.

Setting boundaries can be challenging, especially if you're not used to asserting yourself. Here are practical steps to help you establish and maintain healthy boundaries.

1. Identify Your Limits: Reflect on your values, needs, and preferences. What are your physical, emotional, and mental limits? Understanding your limits is the first step to setting boundaries.

2. Communicate Clearly: Clearly express your boundaries to others. Use assertive but respectful language. For example, instead of saying, "I guess I could stay late," say, "I need to leave by 6 PM to maintain my commitments."

3. Be Consistent: Consistency is key to maintaining boundaries. Once you've set a boundary, stick to it. Inconsistency can confuse others and weaken your resolve.

4. Learn to Say No and Be Unapologetic about It: Practice saying no without feeling guilty. Understand that saying no to others means saying yes to yourself and your well-being. You don't need to provide lengthy explanations and you don't need anybody's stamp of approval. A simple "No, thank you" is sufficient. And it is your right.

5. Use "I" Statements Often: When communicating your boundaries, use "I" statements to express your needs without blaming or accusing others. For example, "I feel overwhelmed when I'm asked to work extra hours. I need to stick to my scheduled work hours to stay balanced."

6. Anticipate Pushback and Remain Resolute: Some people may not respect your boundaries initially. Be prepared for pushback and stay firm in your decisions. Reiterate your boundaries if necessary and stand by them come what may.

Real-Life Scenarios

Here are some scenarios where setting boundaries led to positive changes in people's lives as they strive to remain true to their core values, beliefs and identities.

Chibuchi's Work-Life Balance: Chibuchi, a marketing manager, often found herself working late hours to impress her boss. This took a toll on her personal life and health. Chibuchi decided to set boundaries by clearly communicating her work hours and sticking to them. She also delegated tasks and prioritized her workload. As a result, she achieved a better work-life balance and felt more energized and productive.

Dmytro's Social Boundaries: Dmytro, a college student, felt pressured to attend every social event and gathering. This left him exhausted and affected his academic performance. Dmytro set boundaries by limiting his social engagements to weekends and prioritizing his studies during the week. He explained his decision to his friends, who respected his need for balance. This change allowed Dmytro to excel academically while still enjoying his social life.

Aisha's Family Dynamics: Aisha, a mother of two, often felt overwhelmed by her extended family's demands and expectations. She realized she needed to set boundaries to protect her well-being. Aisha communicated her limits to her family, explaining that she needed time for herself and her immediate family. She also set specific times for family visits and gatherings. This helped reduce her stress and improved her relationship with her extended family.

These examples demonstrate the positive impact of setting boundaries in your personal and workplace relationships. By clearly defining and communicating your limits, you can create a healthier and more genuine life.

Conclusion

In this chapter, we've discussed the importance of setting boundaries, I provided practical steps to help you establish and maintain them. Never forget that boundaries are essential for protecting your well-being, maintaining an authentic lifestyle, and building respectful relationships. By identifying your limits, communicating clearly, being consistent, and learning to say no, you can create a life that reflects your true self and priorities.

In the next chapter, we will explore the need to build healthy relationships. We'll discuss how to recognize toxic relationships and nurture positive connections. I will also share with you case studies of individuals who have improved their relationships by focusing on authenticity and mutual respect.

TIME FOR ACTION

Unlock the power of personal growth with our expert-guided courses. Start your journey to a better you today!

Chapter 8: Developing Healthy Relationships

How to Recognize Toxic Relationships

Healthy relationships are vital for building a fulfilling life that truly reflects who you are. This is why it's essential to recognize and address toxic relationships that can drain your energy, undermine your self-worth and render you a pale shadow of your true self. Here are some signs of toxic relationships.

1. Lack of Support: In a toxic relationship, the other person is unsupportive, dismissive, or even sabotage your efforts and achievements.

2. Constant Criticism: Instead of offering constructive feedback, a toxic person frequently criticizes you in a hurtful and counter-productive manner.

3. Manipulation: Toxic individuals often manipulate others to get what they want, using guilt, deception, or coercion.

4. Control Freaks: They try to control your actions, decisions, and even your thoughts, making you feel restricted, powerless and dependent.

5. Neglect of Boundaries: A toxic person disregards your boundaries, showing little respect for your toils, needs and preferences.

6. Emotional Drain: Every interaction with a toxic person leaves you feeling slighted, drained, anxious, and unhappy.

Nurturing Positive Connections

Once you recognize toxic relationships, your next step must be to focus on nurturing positive connections that support your growth and authenticity. Here are some strategies for building healthy relationships that serve your needs and help you remain who you are.

1. Mutual Respect: Healthy relationships are built on mutual respect. Value each other's opinions, needs, and boundaries.

2. Open Communication: Encourage open and honest communication. Share your thoughts and feelings without fear of judgment, and listen actively to the other person.

3. Empathy and Understanding: Practice empathy by trying to understand things from the other person's perspective. This helps build a deeper emotional connection.

4. Support and Encouragement: Be supportive and encouraging in your dealings with others. Whether it is a love relationship, a multi-family setting, a business partnership or an office environment, learn to celebrate one another's successes and offer help during challenging times.

5. Build Trust: Trust is the foundation of any healthy relationship. Be reliable and trustworthy, and avoid actions that could break trust.

6. Shared Values and Interests: Build connections based on shared values and interests. Engage in activities that everyone truly enjoys and finds meaningful.

Case Studies

Let's look at some examples of individuals who have developed healthy relationships as a means to get rid of the need to seek external approval.

Alex's Friendship Shift: Alex realized that his friend, Sam, was constantly criticizing and manipulating him. After a difficult conversation, Alex decided to distance himself from Sam and focus on friends who were supportive and respectful. So rather than trying to impress Sam, he built stronger bonds with friends who shared his interests and values. His choice helped him achieve a life that aligns with his true self.

Dede's Workplace Boundaries: Dede worked in a toxic environment where her colleagues often undermined her. She decided to set clear boundaries and communicate openly about her needs. She also sought out colleagues who valued collaboration and respect. Over time, Dede formed a supportive network at work, which improved her job satisfaction and performance.

Tom and Vera's Marriage: Tom and Vera realized that their marriage was suffering due to a constant need on Tom's part to seek Vera's approval in every step he takes. After a frank discussion, they realized Tom's faked life was not helping their relationship goals. They sought couples therapy to work on their issues and learned to respect each other's values while celebrating their shared aspirations. By focusing on their shared values and supporting each other's growth, they rebuilt their relationship on a foundation of trust and respect.

These examples highlight the importance of recognizing toxic relationships and nurturing positive connections. By focusing on mutual respect, open communication, empathy, and shared values, you can build healthy relationships that support your authenticity and well-being.

Conclusion

In this chapter, we've learned the importance of developing healthy relationships in our quest for a life that does not need to impress anyone. I showed you strategies for recognizing toxic relationships and building positive connections. Additionally, you've learnt that being your true self through healthy relationships requires mutual respect, open communication, empathy, support, and trust. By focusing on these principles, you can create relationships that help you realize the authentic life you've always wanted.

In the next few chapters, we will delve into the exciting topic of Intentional Living. I will show you how a decision to lead a more purpose-driven life can immensely boost your chances of becoming who you've been created to be. The first step is to understand what intentional living means. Let's do it.

TIME FOR ACTION

Unlock the power of personal growth with our expert-guided courses. Start your journey to a better you today!

PART 4: DISCOVERING INTENTIONAL LIVING Chapters 9 - 16

Chapter 9: The Meaning of Intentional Living

What Is Intentional Living?

Intentional living is a lifestyle that involves making conscious, deliberate choices that align with your values, passions, and purpose. Instead of reacting to external pressures or societal expectations, intentional living encourages you to reflect on what truly matters to you and to live in a way that is authentic and fulfilling.

Key Principles of Intentional Living

Intentional living is built on several core principles that guide the individual in creating a life that reflects their true self. These principles serve as the foundation for making mindful decisions to foster a sense of purpose and contentment.

1. Self-Awareness: Knowing your values, strengths, weaknesses, and passions. Self-awareness is the cornerstone of intentional living, as it helps you make decisions that resonate with your true self.

2. Purposeful Actions: Taking deliberate actions that align with your values and goals. This involves setting clear intentions and making choices that support your long-term vision.

3. Mindfulness: Being present and fully engaged in the moment. Mindfulness helps you appreciate the here and now, rather than being preoccupied with past regrets or future anxieties.

4. Simplicity: Focusing on what truly matters and eliminating unnecessary distractions. Simplifying your life can help you prioritize your values and reduce the noise that comes from external pressures.

5. Authenticity: Being true to yourself and embracing your unique qualities. Authenticity involves letting go of the need to impress others and living in a way that reflects your genuine self.

Benefits of Intentional Living

Most people who adopt an intentional lifestyle experience numerous benefits,

1. Greater Fulfilment: Living in alignment with your values and passions brings a deep sense of satisfaction and contentment.

2. Improved Mental Health: The reduction in the pressure to impress others that comes with intentional living can alleviate stress, anxiety, and depression.

3. Stronger Relationships: Intentional living creates room for building connections based on authenticity and mutual respect. This often leads to deeper, more meaningful relationships.

4. Enhanced Focus: Prioritizing what truly matters helps you avoid distractions. As you stay focused on your goals, you're able to achieve your personal goals.

5. Increased Resilience: Living intentionally builds inner strength and resilience, enabling you to navigate challenges with a clear sense of purpose.

Techniques for Mindfulness and Self-Awareness

Developing mindfulness and self-awareness is essential for intentional living. Here are some techniques to help you cultivate these qualities:

1. Meditation: Regular meditation practice can help you become more aware of your thoughts, feelings, and behaviours. Even a few minutes of daily meditation can improve mindfulness and self-awareness.

2. Journaling: Writing down your thoughts and experiences can provide insights into your values, goals, and patterns. Journaling helps you reflect on your actions and allows you to make conscious choices.

3. Mindful Breathing: Practise mindful breathing. It will help you stay present and reduce stress. Focus on your breath, noticing each inhale and exhale without judgment.

4. Body Scan: A body scan meditation involves paying attention to the sensations in different parts of your body. This practice can help you become more attuned to your physical and emotional state.

5. Gratitude Practice: Regularly expressing gratitude for the positive aspects of your life can shift your focus from external validation to internal fulfilment. Consider keeping a gratitude journal or sharing your appreciation with others.

Case Study: Akio's Journey

Akio, a 45-year-old engineer from Japan, lived a high-pressure life working long hours at a prestigious company. Despite his success, Akio felt unfulfilled and disconnected from his true self. The constant pressure to perform and impress his colleagues left him exhausted and unhappy.

One day, Akio decided to take a break from his demanding job and travel to a remote village in the Japanese countryside. During his stay, he discovered the beauty of a simpler, more intentional lifestyle. He spent his days meditating, practising traditional crafts, and connecting with the local community.

This experience was transformative for Akio. He realized that his true passions lay in creativity and connection, not in climbing the corporate ladder. Upon returning to the city, Akio made significant changes to his life. He left his high-pressure job and started a small business crafting handmade goods. He also began teaching mindfulness and meditation workshops, sharing his journey with others.

Today, Akio feels more fulfilled and at peace than ever before. His journey towards intentional living has brought him a sense of purpose and contentment that he had never experienced in his previous life.

Exercises to Start Living Intentionally

To begin your journey towards intentional living, try the following exercises:

1. Value Exploration: Make a list of your core values. Consider what truly matters to you and why. Reflect on how your current actions align with these values.

2. Vision Board: Create a vision board that represents your goals, dreams, and values. Use images, quotes, and symbols that inspire you. Place it somewhere visible to remind you of your intentions.

3. Daily Intentions: Start each day by setting a clear intention. Decide how you want to feel and what you want to accomplish. Write down your intention and revisit it throughout the day.

4. Mindful Listening: Practise mindful listening in your interactions with others. Give your full attention to the person speaking, without interrupting or thinking about your response. This fosters deeper connections and enhances your mindfulness.

5. Simplify Your Environment: Declutter your physical space by removing items that don't serve a purpose or bring you joy. A simpler environment can help you focus on what truly matters.

Final Thoughts

Your decision to practise intentional living is a powerful step towards breaking free from the cycle of impressing others. As you direct your energy to self-awareness, purposeful actions, mindfulness, simplicity, and authenticity, you can create a life that reflects your true values and passions.

Remember that intentional living is an ongoing process, but each mindful choice you make brings you closer to a more fulfilling and authentic life. As you continue to explore and practise these principles, you will find greater peace, happiness, and a deeper connection with yourself and others.

TIME FOR ACTION

Unlock the power of personal growth with our expert-guided courses. Start your journey to a better you today!

Chapter 10: Identifying Your True Values

The Importance of Knowing Your Values

Identifying your true values is a crucial step in living intentionally. Your values are the guiding principles that shape your decisions, actions, and overall direction in life.

They reflect what is most important to you and help you stay true to yourself. When you are clear about your values, you can make choices that align with your authentic self and lead to greater fulfilment and purpose.

Exercises to Identify Your Core Values

Here are some exercises you can try to help you discover your core values.

1. Reflect on Peak Experiences: Think about times in your life when you felt most fulfilled, happy, and proud. What were you doing? Who were you with? What values were being honoured in those moments? Write down the values that come to mind.

2. Identify Your Role Models: Consider people you admire and respect. What qualities do they possess that you find inspiring? These qualities often reflect your own values. Make a list of these qualities and see which ones resonate most with you.

3. Evaluate Your Passions and Interests: Reflect on the activities, hobbies, and interests that bring you joy and satisfaction. What do these passions say about your values? For example, if you love volunteering, you might value compassion and service.

4. Analyse Your Choices: Look at the major decisions you've made in your life, such as career choices, relationships, and lifestyle changes. What values influenced these decisions? Write down the values that guided you.

5. Consider Your Dislikes: Think about situations, behaviours, or experiences that frustrate or upset you. What values are being violated in these instances? Identifying what you don't value can help clarify what you do value.

Case Study: Afi's Discovery

Afi, a 29-year-old teacher from Togo, felt unfulfilled despite having a stable job and a comfortable life. She realized she was living according to others' expectations rather than her own values. To identify her true values, Afi took a weekend retreat focused on self-discovery and reflection.

During the retreat, Afi participated in various exercises designed to uncover her core values. She reflected on her peak experiences and realized that moments spent with her family and helping her students brought her the most joy. She identified values such as family, education, and compassion. Afi also recognized that her role models were individuals who prioritized these same values.

With this newfound clarity, Afi decided to make changes in her life. She began volunteering at a local community centre, focusing on educational programs for underprivileged children. She also made more time for family gatherings and deepened her connections with loved ones. By aligning her actions with her values, Afi found greater fulfilment and purpose in her life.

Aligning Actions with Values

Once you have identified your core values, the next step is to align your actions with these values. Here's how you can do it.

1. Set Value-Based Goals: Create goals that reflect your values. For example, if you value health, set a goal to exercise regularly and eat nutritious foods. If you value creativity, set a goal to start a new artistic project.

2. Make Conscious Choices: Before making decisions, ask yourself if the choice aligns with your values. This can help you stay true to yourself and avoid actions that don't reflect your authentic self.

3. Create a Personal Value Statement: Write a personal value statement that encapsulates your core values and how you want to live. Refer to this statement regularly to remind yourself of what matters most. You might want to memorize it and recite it to yourself frequently.

4. Prioritize Your Values: Life can be busy and demanding, making it easy to lose sight of your values. Make a conscious effort to prioritize your values in your daily routine. Schedule time for activities that honour your values and eliminate those that don't.

5. Evaluate and Adjust: Regularly evaluate your actions and choices to ensure they align with your values. If you find yourself straying, take steps to realign and make adjustments as needed.

Personal Story: Javier's Realignment

Javier, a 40-year-old entrepreneur from Spain, built a successful tech company but felt increasingly disconnected from his true self. He realized his work was consuming him, leaving little time for his family and personal interests. Javier decided to realign his actions with his values.

He identified his core values as family, adventure, and integrity. To honour these values, Javier made significant changes to his lifestyle. He delegated more responsibilities at work to free up time for family activities and travel. He also committed to being more transparent and ethical in his business practices, ensuring his company operated with integrity.

By realigning his actions with his values, Javier experienced a profound sense of fulfilment. He built stronger relationships with his family, explored new adventures, and felt proud of the ethical standards he set for his business.

Challenges in Living According to Your Values

Living according to your values can be challenging, especially when external pressures and societal expectations conflict with your true desires. Here are some common challenges and how to overcome them:

1. External Pressures: Societal norms, peer pressure, and family expectations can make it difficult to stay true to your values. Overcome this by setting boundaries and communicating your values clearly to others. Seek support from those who respect and encourage your authentic self.

2. Fear of Judgment: The fear of being judged or criticized can deter you from living according to your values. Remember that your values are unique to you, and not everyone will understand or agree with them. Focus on what brings you fulfilment and surround yourself with supportive individuals.

3. Time Constraints: Balancing responsibilities and obligations can make it challenging to prioritize your values. Overcome this by scheduling dedicated time for activities that honour your values and delegating or eliminating tasks that don't.

4. Self-Doubt: Doubting your ability to live according to your values can hold you back. Overcome this by building self-confidence through small, value-based actions. Celebrate your successes and remind yourself of the positive impact of living authentically.

Final Thoughts

Identifying and living according to your true values is a powerful step towards getting rid of the need to impress others unnecessarily through intentional living. By understanding what truly matters to you and aligning your actions with these values, you can create a life that is authentic, fulfilling, and purposeful. Follow the path of self-discovery and value alignment, and remember that each step you take brings you closer to living a life that genuinely reflects who you are.

TIME FOR ACTION

Unlock the power of personal growth with our expert-guided courses. Start your journey to a better you today!

Chapter 11: Setting Intentional Goals

The Importance of Intentional Goals

Setting intentional goals is a critical component of living an authentic and fulfilling life. Unlike goals set to impress others or meet societal expectations, intentional goals are deeply connected to your core values and personal aspirations. They provide direction, motivation, and a clear path to achieving what truly matters to you.

Understanding SMART Goals

One effective framework for setting intentional goals is the SMART criteria, which ensures your goals are **Specific, Measurable, Achievable, Relevant, and Time-bound.** Let me explain further.

1. Specific: Clearly define what you want to achieve. Vague goals can lead to confusion and lack of direction. For example, instead of saying, "I want to be healthier," specify, "I want to exercise for 30 minutes, five times a week."

2. Measurable: Establish criteria for tracking progress and success. This allows you to stay motivated and adjust your approach as needed. For instance, "I want to lose 10 pounds in three months" provides a measurable target.

3. Achievable: Set realistic goals that challenge you but are attainable. Overly ambitious goals can lead to frustration and burnout. Consider your current circumstances and resources when setting any goal.

4. Relevant: Ensure your goals align with your values and long-term aspirations. This relevance keeps you focused and committed. For example, if you value family time, a goal to "spend two hours of quality time with family each day" is relevant.

5. Time-bound: Set a deadline to create a sense of urgency and accountability. A timeframe helps you stay on track and measure progress. For example, "I will complete a 5K run by the end of the year."

Balance Long-term and Short-term Goals

Balancing long-term and short-term goals is essential for maintaining motivation and achieving sustained progress. Long-term goals provide a vision for the future, while short-term goals break that vision into manageable steps.

1. Long-term Goals: These are overarching aspirations that may take months or years to achieve. They reflect your broader values and life purpose. For example, "Start my own business within the next five years" is a long-term goal.

2. Short-term Goals: These are actionable steps that lead to your long-term goals. They are achievable in a shorter timeframe, such as days, weeks, or months. For example, "Complete a business plan within the next three months" is a short-term goal that supports the long-term goal of starting a business.

Case Study: Amandeep's Goal-Setting

Amandeep, a 33-year-old software developer from India, felt unfulfilled despite his successful career. He realized his true passion lay in health and fitness, a value that had been overshadowed by his demanding job. Amandeep decided to set intentional goals that aligned with his passion.

Using the SMART framework, Amandeep set a long-term goal to become a certified fitness trainer within two years. He broke this down into short-term goals:

Specific: Research certification programs within the next month.

Measurable: Enroll in a certification course by the end of the second month.

Achievable: Dedicate two hours each weekend to studying course materials.

Relevant: Incorporate fitness training into his daily routine to stay motivated.

Time-bound: Complete the certification program within 18 months.

By setting these intentional goals, Amandeep successfully transitioned to a career that aligned with his values and brought him greater fulfilment.

How to Overcome Obstacles in Goal Setting

Setting intentional goals is not without challenges. Here are some common obstacles and the strategies to overcome them.

1. Procrastination: Break tasks into smaller, manageable steps to help combat procrastination. Set deadlines for each step to maintain momentum.

2. Fear of Failure: Reframe failure as a learning opportunity. Adopt a growth mindset and understand that setbacks are part of the journey towards success.

3. Lack of Motivation: Connect your goals to your core values to maintain motivation. Visualize the positive impact achieving your goals will have on your life.

4. Distractions: Identify and minimize distractions that derail your focus. Create a dedicated workspace and establish routines to stay on track.

5. Overwhelm: Prioritize your goals and focus on one or two at a time. Break them into smaller tasks to avoid feeling overwhelmed.

Personal Story: Isabella's Journey

Isabella, a 40-year-old artist from Italy, struggled with setting goals after her art gallery closed due to economic downturns. She felt lost and unsure of her next steps. Isabella decided to adopt intentional living by setting goals that aligned with her passion for art and creativity.

She set a long-term goal to reopen her gallery within two years. Her short-term goals included:

Specific: Research online platforms to sell her art within one month.

Measurable: Create and upload five new artworks to the platform each month.

Achievable: Dedicate three hours each day to creating art and managing her online store.

Relevant: Attend local art events to network and gain inspiration.

Time-bound: Launch her online store within six months.

Isabella's intentional goals reignited her passion for art and provided a clear path to achieving her dream. By focusing on her values and breaking her vision into actionable steps, she overcame her uncertainty and found renewed purpose.

How to Create a Goal-Setting Plan

To set intentional goals, follow these steps

1. Reflect on Your Values: Identify your core values and passions. What truly matters to you?

2. Define Your Vision: Create a clear vision of what you want to achieve. Consider both long-term and short-term aspirations.

3. Use the SMART Framework: Apply the SMART criteria to set specific, measurable, achievable, relevant, and time-bound goals.

4. Break Goals into Tasks: Divide your goals into smaller, actionable tasks. Create a timeline for completing each task.

5. Monitor Progress: Regularly review your progress and adjust your plan as needed. Celebrate your achievements and learn from setbacks.

Final Thoughts

A powerful way to align your actions with your values is to set intentional goals. When you appreciate the importance of intentional goals, apply the SMART framework, balance long-term and short-term aspirations, and are able to overcome obstacles, you will achieve what truly matters to you. You can start off on your path of intentional goal setting today and watch as your life transforms into one that reflects your authentic self and brings you genuine happiness.

TIME FOR ACTION

Unlock the power of personal growth with our expert-guided courses. Start your journey to a better you today!

Chapter 12: The Importance of Resisting Societal Pressures

The Need to Recognize External Influences

Societal pressures are pervasive and can significantly impact your decisions and behaviours, often without you realizing it. These pressures come from various sources, including cultural norms, media, family expectations, and peer influence.

The first step towards resisting these external influences as part of your dream for a purpose-driven lifestyle is to identify and know them for what they are and can do to you.

1. Cultural Norms: Societal expectations regarding success, beauty, and behaviour can shape your actions and beliefs. Cultural norms often dictate what is considered acceptable or desirable, leading you to conform even if it conflicts with your values.

2. Media Influence: Television, social media, and advertising constantly bombard you with messages about what you must have and how you should look, behave, and live. These messages can create unrealistic standards and perpetuate the need to impress others.

3. Family Expectations: Family members often have expectations about our careers, relationships, and lifestyle. While their intentions may be harmless, these expectations can pressure you to make choices that don't align with your true desires. And they may not like what you eventually become by succumbing to their pressures.

The sad thing is that these 'loving' family people might never realize their contribution to your failures. They will blame it all on you alone.

4. Peer Influence: Friends and colleagues can exert significant influence over your decisions. The desire to fit in or gain approval from your social circle can lead you to compromise your authenticity.

How to Build Resistance Against Societal Pressures

Developing resilience against societal pressures is crucial for living intentionally. Here are strategies to help you stay true to yourself:

1. Self-Reflection: Regularly reflect on your values, goals, and desires. Understand what truly matters to you and why. Self-awareness helps you recognize when external pressures are influencing your decisions.

2. Set Boundaries: Establish clear boundaries to protect your values and well-being. Learn to say no to activities or commitments that don't align with your priorities.

3. Limit Media Consumption: Be mindful of the media you consume. Reduce exposure to content that promotes unrealistic standards or makes you feel inadequate. Curate your social media feeds to include positive, inspiring content.

4. Seek Support: Surround yourself with people who respect and support your values. Build a network of friends, mentors, and family members who encourage you and are happy with you being your authentic self.

5. Practice Mindfulness: Engage in mindfulness practices such as meditation, journaling, or yoga to stay grounded and present. Mindfulness helps you stay connected to your true self amidst external pressures.

Illustration: Life Driven by Societal

Expectations vs. Intentional Living

Consider the illustration below. It will help you picture the impact of societal pressures and the benefits of intentional living.

1. Life Driven by Societal Expectations

Here are the characteristics of such a lifestyle.

External Validation: You constantly seek approval from others.

Inauthentic Choices: You make decisions based on what is expected rather than what you truly want.

Stress and Anxiety: You feel overwhelmed by the need to meet societal standards.

Shallow Relationships: Most connections you build are based on impressing others.

Lack of Fulfilment: You experience a sense of emptiness and dissatisfaction much of the time.

2. Life Guided by Intentional Living Principles

Here are the major characteristics of this type of lifestyle.

Internal Fulfilment: You find satisfaction in aligning with your values.

Authentic Choices: You make decisions that reflect your true desires.

Peace and Contentment: You feel at ease with your choices and lifestyle.

Deep Relationships: You easily build genuine connections based on mutual respect and understanding.

True Fulfilment: You experience a sense of purpose and contentment.

Case Study: Liz's Transformation

Liz, a 37-year-old lawyer from the United Kingdom, struggled with the pressure to meet societal and familial expectations. Despite her successful career, she felt unfulfilled and stressed. Liz realized that her career choice was heavily influenced by her family's expectations and societal norms about success.

Determined to live more intentionally, Liz took a sabbatical to explore her true passions. She discovered a love for environmental conservation and decided to pursue a career in this field. Liz faced resistance from her family and peers, but she stayed committed to her values.

She set boundaries by limiting discussions about her career change with unsupportive family members and sought out a supportive community of like-minded individuals.

Liz also practised mindfulness through daily meditation and nature walks, helping her stay grounded and connected to her true self.

Today, Liz works for a non-profit organization dedicated to environmental conservation. She feels fulfilled and content, knowing that her work aligns with her values and passions.

Liz's transformation illustrates the power of overcoming societal pressures and living intentionally.

Strategies to Resist Societal Pressures

Here are additional strategies you can implement to help you resist societal pressures and stay true to your values.

1. Develop a Strong Sense of Self: Cultivate self-confidence and a clear understanding of your identity. The more secure you are in who you are, the less likely you are to be swayed by external influences.

2. Practice Assertiveness: Learn to communicate your needs, desires, and boundaries assertively. Stand up for yourself and express your values without apology.

3. Create a Vision Board: Visualize your goals and values by creating a vision board. Display it prominently to remind yourself of your intentions and keep you focused.

4. Engage in Self-Care: Prioritize self-care activities that nurture your mind, body, and spirit. Self-care helps you maintain balance and resilience against external pressures.

5. Reflect on Your Progress: Regularly assess your progress towards living intentionally. Celebrate your achievements and identify areas for improvement.

Personal Story: Daniel's Journey

Daniel, a 28-year-old graphic designer from the United States, felt immense pressure to follow a conventional career path. Despite his passion for art and design, he pursued a degree in business administration to meet societal expectations of success.

After years of working in a corporate job, Daniel felt unfulfilled and disconnected from his true self. He decided to take a leap of faith and follow his passion for graphic design. Daniel enrolled in design courses, built a portfolio, and eventually launched his own freelance business.

To resist societal pressures, Daniel practised assertiveness by clearly communicating his career change to his family and peers. He limited exposure to media that glorified corporate success and focused on building a supportive community of fellow creatives.

Daniel's journey was challenging, but his commitment to living intentionally paid off. He now enjoys a fulfilling career that aligns with his values and passions, and he feels more authentic and content than ever before.

Final Thoughts

The ability to decisively ward off societal pressures is essential for living an intentional and authentic life. You will only make choices that reflect your true self if you can recognize external influences, build resilience, and stay committed to your values. Work with the strategies and stories shared in this chapter to empower yourself to resist societal pressures and create a life that genuinely fulfils you. Always remember this: The journey may be challenging, but the rewards of living intentionally are immeasurable.

TIME FOR ACTION

Unlock the power of personal growth with our expert-guided courses. Start your journey to a better you today!

Chapter 13: Choosing Authenticity in Relationships

The Importance of Authenticity in Relationships

Authenticity is the foundation of meaningful and lasting relationships. When you are true to yourself, you build connections based on mutual respect, trust, and understanding. Authentic relationships bring joy, support, and a sense of belonging. They allow you to be vulnerable, share your true feelings, and grow together with others.

The Role of Open Communication

Open communication is necessary for authenticity in relationships. It involves expressing your thoughts, feelings and needs honestly and respectfully. Here are some key aspects of open communication:

1. Honesty: Be truthful about your feelings, experiences, and perspectives. Avoid hiding or distorting the truth to impress others or avoid conflict.

2. Transparency: Share your intentions, expectations, and boundaries. Transparency helps prevent misunderstandings and builds trust.

3. Active Listening: Listen attentively to others without interrupting or judging. Show empathy and validate their feelings. Active listening fosters mutual respect and understanding.

4. Constructive Feedback: Give and receive feedback with an open mind. Offer feedback in a supportive manner and be willing to accept criticism gracefully.

How to Build Genuine Connections

Building genuine connections requires effort and intention. Here are some ways to cultivate authentic relationships:

1. Be Yourself: Learn to feel proud of your true self and let others see who you are. Authenticity attracts like-minded individuals who appreciate and accept you for who you are.

2. Show Vulnerability: Do not be afraid to share your struggles, fears, and insecurities. Vulnerability creates deeper bonds and encourages others to open up as well.

3. Support Others: Be there for your friends and loved ones. Offer help, encouragement, and a listening ear. Genuine support strengthens relationships.

4. Shared Experiences: Engage in activities and experiences that you and your friends enjoy. Shared experiences create lasting memories and strengthen connections.

5. Respect Differences: Appreciate and respect the differences in others. Embrace diversity and learn from each other's unique perspectives.

Personal Story: Benyiwa's Rebuilding

Benyiwa, a 34-year-old marketing manager from Ghana, realized that many of her relationships were based on impressing others. She felt disconnected and lonely despite having a large social circle. Benyiwa decided to practise authenticity and rebuild her relationships.

She started by being honest about her feelings and experiences. Instead of pretending to have everything under control, she shared her struggles and insecurities with her close friends. To her surprise, they responded with empathy and support.

Benyiwa also made an effort to listen actively and show genuine interest in others' lives. She organized small gatherings and activities that reflected her true interests. Over time, Sophia built deeper, more meaningful connections with her friends. She felt more supported and understood, and her relationships brought her genuine joy.

Case Study: Amit Accepts His Vulnerability

Amit, a 40-year-old engineer from India, struggled with expressing his emotions. He believed that showing vulnerability was a sign of weakness. This belief affected his relationships, as he often hid his true feelings and avoided deep conversations.

Determined to change, Amit began practising vulnerability. He started by sharing small, personal stories with his friends and family. Gradually, he opened up about his fears, dreams, and challenges. Amit found that being vulnerable strengthened his relationships. His friends and family appreciated his honesty and responded with their own stories and support.

Amit's journey taught him that vulnerability is a strength that fosters connection and trust. As a result of his new authentic lifestyle, he built deeper and more meaningful relationships.

Dealing with Challenges in Relationships

Building authentic relationships can be challenging. This is especially so if you have been conditioned by your upbringing to hide your true self. Here are some common challenges and strategies to overcome them.

1. Fear of Rejection: The fear of being rejected or judged can prevent you from being authentic. Overcome this by building self-confidence and understanding that true friends will accept you as you are.

2. Past Hurts: Previous experiences of betrayal or rejection can make it difficult to trust others. Heal from past hurts by seeking therapy, practicing self-care, and gradually opening up to others.

3. Societal Norms: Societal expectations may pressure you to conform and hide your true self. Resist this by staying true to your values and surrounding yourself with supportive, like-minded individuals.

4. Communication Barriers: Effective communication requires practice. Improve your communication skills through active listening, assertiveness training, and seeking feedback.

How to Be Your Authentic Self in Different Types of Relationships

1. Family Relationships: Family dynamics can be complex, but authenticity is crucial for healthy family relationships. Practice open communication, set boundaries, and show empathy and understanding.

2. Friendships: Build friendships based on mutual respect, support, and shared interests. Be yourself and encourage your friends to do the same.

3. Romantic Relationships: Authenticity is essential for intimacy and trust in romantic relationships. Be open about your feelings, needs, and boundaries. Support each other's growth at every opportunity.

4. Professional Relationships: While professional settings may require a certain level of formality, authenticity can still play a role.

Be honest about your capabilities, seek feedback, and build genuine connections with colleagues.

Case Study: Zuri's Reconnection with Authenticity

Zuri, a 28-year-old artist from Uganda, felt disconnected from her family due to their differing views and expectations. She often pretended to agree with them to avoid conflict, but this left her feeling isolated and misunderstood.

Determined to reconnect authentically, Zuri decided to have an open conversation with her family. She expressed her true feelings and values, and listened to their perspectives without judgment. Although the conversation was challenging, it led to greater understanding and respect.

Zuri's family appreciated her honesty, and they worked together to find common ground. By embracing authenticity, Zuri rebuilt her relationship with her family on a foundation of mutual respect and understanding.

Final Thoughts

Developing authenticity in relationships is a powerful way to build deeper, more meaningful connections. By practising open communication, showing vulnerability, and being true to yourself, you can create relationships that bring joy, support, and a sense of belonging.

Also, overcoming challenges and building authenticity in different types of relationships takes effort and commitment, but the rewards are immeasurable. Authentic relationships enrich your life and help you stay true to your values and aspirations, leading to a more fulfilling and intentional life.

TIME FOR ACTION

Unlock the power of personal growth with our expert-guided courses. Start your journey to a better you today!

Chapter 14: The Benefits of a Simplified Life

Today, we live in a materialistic world filled with constant noise, distractions, and obligations. The pressure on you and me to conform and win approval keeps growing. You've already seen the effects of all these on mental and physical health. This is why a simplified life can bring immense benefits.

Essential steps to a simplified life include decluttering your physical space, streamlining your commitments, and focusing on what truly matters. This process will bring minimal stress, increased clarity, and a greater sense of peace and fulfilment.

How to Declutter Your Physical Space

A cluttered environment can contribute to a cluttered mind. Here are some steps to help you declutter your physical space:

1. Assess Your Space: Take a close look at your home or workspace. Identify areas that feel cluttered or chaotic.

2. Sort and Categorize: Divide your belongings into these categories: keep, donate, sell, and discard. Be honest about what you truly need and use.

3. Start Small: Begin with one area or room at a time to avoid being overwhelmed. Even small progress can make a significant difference.

4. Organize Mindfully: Arrange your belongings in a way that makes sense and is easy to maintain. Use storage solutions that help keep things tidy and accessible.

5. Regular Maintenance: Set aside time each week or month to maintain your decluttered space. Regular upkeep prevents clutter from accumulating again.

Adopt a Minimalist Lifestyle

Minimalism is a lifestyle that promotes living with less to focus on what truly matters. It's not about depriving yourself but rather about doing away with needless extras and living with intention. Here are some principles of minimalism.

1. Quality Over Quantity: Choose high-quality items that bring you joy and serve a purpose, rather than accumulating unnecessary possessions.

2. Mindful Consumption: Be intentional about what you bring into your life. Before making a purchase, ask yourself if it aligns with your values and if you truly need it.

3. Experiences Over Things: Focus on creating and cherishing experiences rather than acquiring material possessions. Experiences often bring lasting joy and fulfilment.

4. Digital Minimalism: Apply minimalist principles to your digital life. Organize your digital files, unsubscribe from unnecessary emails, and limit screen time to reduce digital clutter.

Case Study: Liam's Journey to Minimalism

Liam, a 37-year-old teacher from Australia, felt overwhelmed by the constant clutter in his home and life. He realized that his possessions were not bringing him happiness and that he was spending too much time maintaining them. Liam decided to embrace minimalism.

He started by decluttering his home, donating items he no longer needed and selling unnecessary gadgets and clothes. Liam focused on keeping only what brought him joy and served a practical purpose. He also applied minimalism to his schedule, cutting down on commitments that didn't align with his values.

As a result, Liam found that he had more time and energy to devote to his passions, such as hiking and spending time with loved ones. His simplified lifestyle brought him greater peace and fulfilment.

How to Streamline Your Commitments

The habit of overcommitting yourself just to please others or win their approval can lead to stress and burnout. When you simplify your commitments you will begin to focus on what truly matters. Here are some steps to streamline your commitments.

1. Evaluate Your Commitments: Make a list of all your current commitments, including work, social, and personal obligations. Assess which ones align with your values and bring you joy.

2. Prioritize: Determine which commitments are most important to you and focus on those. Let go of commitments that don't serve your well-being or align with your values.

3. Learn to Say No: Politely decline new commitments that don't align with your priorities. Saying no allows you to protect your time and energy for what matters most.

4. Delegate and Share Responsibilities: If possible, delegate tasks to others or share responsibilities to lighten your load.

5. Create Boundaries: Set clear boundaries around your time and commitments. Communicate your limits to others and stick to them.

Personal Story: Winnie's Simplified Schedule

Winnie, a 29-year-old nurse from South Africa, struggled with balancing her demanding job, social obligations, and personal interests. She often felt exhausted and stressed. Determined to simplify her life, Winnie decided to streamline her commitments.

Winnie evaluated her schedule and identified activities that didn't align with her values or bring her joy. She politely declined social invitations that felt like obligations rather than genuine connections. Winnie also set boundaries at work, ensuring she had time for self-care and rest.

By simplifying her schedule, Winnie quickly found that she had more time for activities that truly mattered to her, such as volunteering at a local clinic and spending quality time with her family. Her stress levels decreased, and she felt more balanced and fulfilled.

Ways to Find True Happiness in Simplicity

Simplifying your life allows you to find joy in simple pleasures and appreciate the present moment. Here are some ways to embrace simplicity and find happiness.

1. Mindful Living: Practice mindfulness by being present and fully engaged in each moment. Mindful living helps you appreciate the beauty and joy in everyday experiences.

2. Gratitude Practice: Cultivate gratitude by regularly reflecting on what you are thankful for. Gratitude shifts your focus from what you lack to what you have, fostering contentment and happiness.

3. Slow Down: Have a slower pace of life. Take time to enjoy simple activities, such as a walk in nature, reading a book, or spending time with loved ones.

4. Connection with Nature: Spend time in nature to reconnect with its beauty and tranquillity. Nature has a calming effect and can help you feel more grounded and centred.

5. Intentional Activities: Engage in activities that bring you real joy and fulfilment. Focus on hobbies and passions that align with your values and interests.

Case Study: Rita's Joyful Simplicity

Rita, a 42-year-old chef from Jamaica, found herself constantly rushing through life, missing out on simple pleasures. She decided to simplify her life and embrace joy in simplicity.

Rita started by practising mindful living, savouring each moment and being fully present in her daily activities. She also cultivated a gratitude practice, reflecting on things she was thankful for each day. Rita slowed down her pace of life, taking time to enjoy cooking, gardening, and spending time with her family.

By embracing simplicity, Rita found greater joy and fulfilment in her daily life. She felt more connected to herself and her loved ones, and her overall well-being improved.

Practical Tips for Simplifying Your Life

Here are some practical tips to help you simplify your life and focus on what truly matters.

1. Declutter Regularly: Make decluttering a regular practice. Set aside time each month to assess your belongings and let go of what you no longer need.

2. Simplify Your Wardrobe: Create a capsule wardrobe with versatile, high-quality pieces that you love. This reduces decision fatigue and simplifies your daily routine.

3. Limit Screen Time: Set boundaries around your use of technology. Allocate specific times for checking emails and social media, and take regular digital detoxes.

4. Practice Minimalist Decorating: Simplify your home decor by choosing a few meaningful and aesthetically pleasing items. A minimalist space promotes calm and focus.

5. Prioritize Self-Care: Make self-care a priority. Schedule regular time for activities that nurture your mind, body, and spirit.

Final Thoughts

Simplifying your life is an effective way to create space for what truly matters. By decluttering your physical space, embracing minimalism, streamlining your commitments, and finding joy in simplicity, you can reduce stress and increase fulfilment. The principles and strategies shared in this chapter should help you to get out of the approval-seeking trap and focus on what brings you genuine happiness and peace

TIME FOR ACTION

Unlock the power of personal growth with our expert-guided courses. Start your journey to a better you today!

PART 5: SUSTAINING CHANGE
Chapters 15 - 17

Chapter 15: Finding Fulfilment in the Every Day

The Power of Small Moments

Life is made up of countless small moments. Quite often, finding fulfilment simply comes from appreciating these moments rather than constantly chasing grand achievements or milestones. Your decision to actively utilize the power of small moments can transform your daily life, bringing joy, contentment, and a sense of purpose.

Find Joy in Simple Pleasures

Simple pleasures are the everyday moments that bring you joy and contentment. They can be easily overlooked in the hustle and bustle of life, but recognizing and appreciating them can significantly enhance your well-being. Here are some ways to find joy in simple pleasures.

1. Morning Routine: Start your day with a routine that makes you happy. Whether it's enjoying a cup of coffee, meditating, or taking a morning walk, find something that sets a positive tone for your day.

2. Nature: Spend time in nature to connect with its beauty and tranquillity. A walk in the park, gardening on a homestead, or simply sitting outside can bring a sense of peace and joy.

3. Creativity: Engage in creative activities that you enjoy, such as painting, writing, cooking, or playing music. Creativity can be a powerful source of fulfilment.

4. Relationships: Cherish moments with loved ones. A heartfelt conversation, a hug, or spending quality time together can bring deep joy.

5. Mindful Eating: Savour your meals by eating mindfully. Appreciate the flavours, textures, and aromas of your food, and enjoy the experience of nourishing your body.

Express Gratitude Abundantly

Gratitude is a powerful practice that can shift your focus from what you lack to what you have. A habit of unending gratitude gives a sense of contentment and fulfilment. Take the following steps to practice gratitude.

1. Gratitude Journal: Keep a gratitude journal where you write down things you are thankful for each day. This can help you reflect on the positive aspects of your life.

2. Gratitude Meditation: Incorporate gratitude into your meditation practice. Focus on the things you are grateful for and let the feelings of appreciation fill your heart and mind.

3. Thank You Notes: Write thank you notes to people who have made a positive impact on your life. Expressing gratitude to others can strengthen your relationships and enhance your sense of fulfilment.

4. Daily Reflection: Take a few moments each day to reflect on what you are grateful for. This can be done in the morning to set a positive tone for the day or in the evening to end the day on a positive note.

Personal Story: Santiago's Gratitude Practice

Santiago, a 45-year-old nurse from Mexico, felt overwhelmed by the demands of his job and the challenges of daily life. To find more fulfilment, Santiago decided to start a gratitude practice.

He began keeping a gratitude journal, writing down three things he was thankful for each day. At first, it was challenging to find things to be grateful for, but over time, Santiago noticed a shift in his perspective. He started to appreciate the small moments, like a patient's smile, a colleague's support, or a beautiful sunset.

Santiago also incorporated gratitude into his daily meditation practice, focusing on the positive aspects of his life and letting go of stress and negativity. This practice helped Santiago feel more content and fulfilled, even during challenging times.

Practise Mindfulness

Mindfulness is the practice of being present and fully engaged in the moment. It can help you find fulfilment by allowing you to appreciate the here and now, rather than worrying about the past or future. Here are some ways to practise mindfulness.

Please note that we've already said much about mindfulness practice in previous sections.

1. Mindful Breathing: Practise mindful breathing by focusing on your breath. Notice each inhale and exhale, and let your breath anchor you to the present moment.

2. Body Scan: Perform a body scan meditation, paying attention to the sensations in different parts of your body. This practice can help you become more aware of your physical and emotional state.

3. Mindful Walking: Take a walk and focus on the experience of walking. Notice the sensation of your feet on the ground, the sights and sounds around you, and the feeling of the air on your skin.

4. Mindful Listening: Practice mindful listening in your interactions with others. Give your full attention to the person speaking, without interrupting or thinking about your response.

5. Mindful Activities: Engage in everyday activities mindfully, such as eating, washing dishes, or folding laundry. Focus on the sensations and experience of the activity, rather than letting your mind wander.

Case Study: Chunhua's Mindfulness Journey

Chunhua, a 30-year-old teacher from China, struggled with stress and anxiety due to her demanding job. She decided to explore mindfulness as a way to find more fulfilment in her daily life.

Chunhua started practising mindful breathing and body scan meditations each morning. She also incorporated mindfulness into her daily activities, such as eating, walking, and interacting with her students.

By focusing on the present moment, Chunhua found that she was able to reduce her stress and appreciate the small joys in her life.

Chunhua's mindfulness practice also improved her relationships with her students and colleagues. She became a better listener and more patient and compassionate in her interactions. As a result, Chunhua felt more fulfilled and connected in both her personal and professional life.

Establish Meaningful Rituals

Rituals are intentional practices that bring structure, meaning, and joy to your daily life. They can help you find fulfilment by providing moments of reflection, connection, and celebration. Here are some ideas for creating meaningful rituals.

1. Morning Ritual: Start your day with a ritual that sets a positive tone, such as meditation, journaling, or a gratitude practice.

2. Evening Ritual: End your day with a calming ritual, such as reading, reflecting on the day, or practising mindfulness.

3. Mealtime Ritual: Create a ritual around mealtime, such as saying a blessing, expressing gratitude, or sharing highlights of the day with loved ones.

4. Weekly Ritual: Establish a weekly ritual that brings joy and connection, such as a family game night, a nature walk, or a creative project.

5. Seasonal Rituals: Celebrate the changing seasons with rituals that honour nature and the cycles of life, such as planting a garden in spring, enjoying outdoor activities in summer, or cosying up with a good book in winter.

Personal Story: Asuka's Rituals

Asuka, a 59-year-old architect from Japan, felt that her life lacked structure and meaning. To find more fulfilment, Asuka decided to create meaningful rituals.

She started with a morning ritual of meditation and journaling, which helped her set a positive intention for the day. Asuka also established an evening ritual of reading and reflecting on her day, which brought a sense of closure and calm.

Asuka created mealtime rituals by expressing gratitude and sharing highlights of the day with her family. She also established weekly rituals, such as a family hike on weekends and a creative project night. These rituals brought joy, connection, and a sense of purpose to Asuka's life.

Find Purpose in Everyday Tasks

Everyday tasks, such as household chores or work responsibilities, can feel mundane and unfulfilling. However, finding purpose in these tasks can transform them into meaningful activities. Here are some unique ways to find purpose in your everyday tasks.

1. Reframe Your Perspective: Shift your perspective to see everyday tasks as opportunities to care for yourself and others. For example, view cleaning as a way to create a peaceful environment or cooking as a way to nourish your body.

2. Set Intentions: Set intentions for your tasks. Focus on the positive impact they have on your life. For example, set an intention to bring joy to your home through cleaning or to provide a healthy meal through cooking.

3. Practice Mindfulness: Engage in tasks mindfully, paying attention to the sensations and experiences involved. This can help you appreciate the task and find fulfilment in the process.

4. Find Joy in the Process: Look for moments of joy and satisfaction in the process of completing tasks. For example, enjoy the feeling of warm water while washing dishes or the smell of freshly baked bread.

5. Connect Tasks to Your Values: Relate everyday tasks to your core values. For example, if you value health, view exercise as a way to honour that value or if you value family, see household chores as a way to care for your loved ones.

Final Thoughts

Remember that achieving satisfaction in the every day involves appreciating small moments, practising gratitude and mindfulness, creating meaningful rituals, and finding purpose in everyday tasks.

When you direct your mind and energy to these aspects, you can transform your daily life into a source of joy, contentment, and purpose. You will no longer have to live a life based on what others expect from you. Use the strategies and stories shared in this chapter to find fulfilment in the every day and live a more intentional and authentic life. Look at each moment as an opportunity to connect with your true self. This way, you will experience the richness of life.

TIME FOR ACTION

Unlock the power of personal growth with our expert-guided courses. Start your journey to a better you today!

Chapter 16: Creating Lasting Habits

Habit Formation

Lasting habits are essential for sustaining the changes you've made towards living without trying to impress others. Habits are behaviours that become automatic over time. They make it easier to maintain new, positive actions without constant effort. The following guidelines will help you form enduring habits geared towards living intentionally.

1. Start Small: Begin with small, manageable changes that are easy to incorporate into your daily routine. Small habits are less overwhelming and easier to maintain.

2. Be Consistent: Consistency is key to habit formation. Perform the new habit at the same time or in the same context each day to help it become ingrained in your routine.

3. Use Triggers: Pair your new habit with an existing one to create a trigger. For example, if you want to start meditating, do it right after brushing your teeth in the morning.

4. Track Your Progress: Keep a journal or use an app to track your progress. Seeing your consistency over time can be motivating and help you stay on track.

5. Reward Yourself: Reward yourself for maintaining your new habit. Positive reinforcement can make the habit more enjoyable. It thus increases your motivation to continue.

6. Be Patient: Creating and sustaining a new habit takes time. Be patient with yourself and understand that setbacks are normal. Focus on progress rather than perfection.

Consistency and Patience

Consistency and patience are critical factors in creating lasting habits. Here's how to cultivate these qualities.

1. Set Realistic Goals: Set achievable goals that you can consistently meet. Unrealistic goals can lead to frustration and burnout.

2. Celebrate Small Wins: Acknowledge and celebrate your progress, no matter how small. Celebrating small wins keeps you motivated and reinforces positive behaviour.

3. Practice Self-Compassion: Be kind to yourself if you slip up. Rather than being critical, remind yourself that setbacks are a part of the process. Just focus on getting back on track.

4. Visualize Your Success: Imagine yourself successfully maintaining your new habit. This positive imagery can boost your confidence and commitment.

5. Stay Flexible: Be open to adjusting your approach if something isn't working. Flexibility allows you to find what works best for you and sustain your habit over the long term.

Real-Life Examples

There's much to learn from these examples of individuals who have successfully created lasting habits.

Maabena's Exercise Routine: Maabena, a 26-year old musician from Ghana, wanted to incorporate regular exercise into her life. She started with a small goal of walking for 10 minutes each day. As she became consistent, she gradually increased her exercise time and incorporated other activities like yoga and strength training. Maabena tracked her progress and rewarded herself with small treats for her consistency. Over time, exercising became a natural part of her daily routine.

Zixin's Mindfulness Practice: Zixin, a 44-year-old computer programmer from China, struggled with stress and wanted to develop a mindfulness practice. He began with just 5 minutes of meditation each morning, using his morning coffee as a trigger. Zixin used a meditation app to track his sessions and joined a mindfulness community for support. Despite occasional lapses, he remained patient and focused on his progress. Today, mindfulness is a regular part of his life, helping him manage stress effectively.

Eva's Healthy Eating: Eva, a 35-year-old makeup artist from The Netherlands, aimed to improve her diet by eating more vegetables. She started by adding a serving of vegetables to one meal each day. Eva used a habit-tracking app to monitor her intake and rewarded herself with a favourite activity each week she met her goal. She also sought support from friends who shared her commitment to healthy eating. Gradually, healthy eating became a habit, and Eva felt more energetic and vibrant.

These examples illustrate the power of small, consistent steps and the importance of patience in creating lasting habits. By starting small, being consistent, and celebrating progress, you can develop new habits that support your authentic self.

Conclusion

In this chapter, we took a close look at the process of creating lasting habits. We've emphasized the importance of starting small, being consistent, and staying patient. By using triggers, tracking progress, rewarding yourself, and practising self-compassion, you can form new, positive habits that align with your authentic self and support your long-term goals.

TIME FOR ACTION

Unlock the power of personal growth with our expert-guided courses. Start your journey to a better you today!

Chapter 17: 150 Living to Impress vs Intentional Living Quotes

Look here, I've got for you a large collection of inspirational quotes about the subject of living to impress others. They're in three categories namely being your true self, intentional living and self-awareness.

Use them to strengthen your resolve to let go of the tendency to seek approval from others and to begin living in tandem with your core values.

Being Your Real Self, Not Trying to Impress Quotes

1. " If you know how quickly people forget the dead you will stop living to impress people." – Christopher Walken

2. "When you are content to be simply yourself and don't compare or compete, everyone will respect you." – Lao Tzu

3. "You can't please everyone, and you can't make everyone like you." – Katie Couric

4. "Don't change so people will like you. Be yourself and the right people will love the real you." – Anonymous

5. "Trying to impress others is an act of insecurity." – Sai Pradeep

6. "Care about what other people think and you will always be their prisoner." – Lao Tzu

7. "The only person you should try to be better than is the person you were yesterday." – Anonymous

8. "Don't let the noise of others' opinions drown out your own inner voice." – Steve Jobs

9. "The need for approval destroys the desire for freedom." – Tara Brach

10. "Why are you trying so hard to fit in when you were born to stand out?" – Ian Wallace

11. "When you seek approval from others, you are not allowing yourself to be yourself." – Jody Doty

12. "I don't know the key to success, but the key to failure is trying to please everybody." – Bill Cosby

13. "Be yourself, because an original is worth more than a copy." – Anonymous

14. "Do not chase people. Be yourself, do your own thing and work hard. The right people who belong in your life will come to you, and stay." – Wu-Tang

15. "The unhappiest people in this world are those who care the most about what other people think." – C. JoyBell C.

16. "You were born an original. Don't die a copy." – John Mason

17. "Trying to impress others makes us forget who we really are." – Anonymous

18. "Be yourself, everyone else is already taken." – Oscar Wilde

19. "When you stop expecting people to be perfect, you can like them for who they are." – Donald Miller

20. "To be beautiful means to be yourself. You don't need to be accepted by others. You need to accept yourself." – Thich Nhat Hanh

21. "If you live for people's acceptance, you'll die from their rejection." – Lecrae

22. "Your time is limited, so don't waste it living someone else's life." – Steve Jobs

23. "The greatest prison people live in is the fear of what other people think." – David Icke

24. "Don't wait for the approval of others. You've got the knowledge and the approval of yourself." – Tom Bilyeu

25. "You can't go through life trying to please everyone. You'll lose yourself. Don't let anyone make you feel guilty for living your life your way." – Anonymous

26. "It's not your job to like me. It's mine." – Byron Katie

27. "One of the greatest regrets in life is being what others would want you to be, rather than being yourself." – Shannon L. Alder

28. "Don't try to impress others. Let them be impressed by the way you handle your imperfections." – Anonymous

29. "When you give yourself permission to be yourself, you help others be themselves." – Dan Coppersmith

30. "Trying to be someone else is a waste of the person you are." – Kurt Cobain

31. "Don't spend your life trying to impress others. Do what you love and love what you do." – Anonymous

32. "You have been criticizing yourself for years and it hasn't worked. Try approving of yourself and see what happens." – Louise L. Hay

33. "The greatest thing in the world is to know how to belong to oneself." – Michel de Montaigne

34. "Your value doesn't decrease based on someone's inability to see your worth." – Anonymous

35. "Approval from others is fleeting. True contentment comes from within." – Anonymous

36. "You wouldn't worry so much about what others think of you if you realized how seldom they do." – Eleanor Roosevelt

37. "Don't aim to impress others. Aim to impress yourself." – Anonymous

38. "Being true to yourself is better than being a liar just to impress everyone." – Anonymous

39. "The more you try to impress, the less impressed they'll be." – Anonymous

40. "The only approval you need is your own." – Anonymous

41. "Don't let the opinions of others consume you." – Anonymous

42. "The freedom of being yourself is the greatest freedom of all." – Anonymous

43. "Don't waste your time trying to impress people who don't appreciate your true self." – Anonymous

44. "Be yourself. People don't have to like you, and you don't have to care." – Anonymous

45. "When you start doing things because they matter to you, you'll stop caring about impressing others." – Anonymous

46. "The more you let go of trying to impress others, the more your life will improve." – Anonymous

47. "What you think of yourself is much more important than what people think of you." – Anonymous

48. "Your worth is not measured by the opinions of others." – Anonymous

49. "You don't need to impress others. Just be yourself and people will respect you." – Anonymous

50. "Stop caring about impressing others and start impressing yourself." – Anonymous

Intentional Living Quotes

1. "Intentional living is the art of making our own choices before others' choices make us." – Richie Norton

2. "The first step to getting the things you want out of life is this: Decide what you want." – Ben Stein

3. "Living with intention means saying no to the things that aren't important to us so that we can say yes to what matters most." – Anonymous

4. "Live less out of habit and more out of intent." – Anonymous

5. "Your life does not get better by chance, it gets better by change." – Jim Rohn

6. "Intentional living is the antidote to a life on autopilot." – Anonymous

7. "The more intentional you are about your choices, the more meaningful your life becomes." – Anonymous

8. "Purpose is the reason you journey. Passion is the fire that lights your way." – Anonymous

9. "Live with intention. Walk to the edge. Listen hard. Practice wellness. Play with abandon. Laugh." – Mary Anne Radmacher

10. "Intentional living is about knowing why you do what you do and choosing to do it." – Anonymous

11. "Don't wait for everything to be perfect before you decide to enjoy your life." – Joyce Meyer

12. "Decide upon your major definite purpose in life and then organize all your activities around it." – Brian Tracy

13. "Your life is your message to the world. Make sure it's inspiring." – Anonymous

14. "When you live with intention, you create the life you want, rather than the life that happens to you." – Anonymous

15. "To live intentionally implies that it is not only possible to do so, but that we are already living intentionally, in our own way, at our own pace." – Anonymous

16. "In the end, it's not the years in your life that count. It's the life in your years." – Abraham Lincoln

17. "Intentional living is the conscious application of purpose in every day." – Anonymous

18. "Living intentionally means thinking about your decisions instead of just making them. It means knowing your values and making choices that align with them." – Anonymous

19. "Intentional living is the difference between living a life of existence and living a life of purpose." – Anonymous

20. "The secret of success is constancy of purpose." – Benjamin Disraeli

21. "Living with intention is about embracing what you truly want and letting go of what you don't." – Anonymous

22. "The purpose of life is a life of purpose." – Robert Byrne

23. "Be the designer of your world and not merely the consumer of it." – James Clear

24. "You were born with the ability to change someone's life – don't ever waste it." – Dale Partridge

25. "Life isn't about finding yourself. Life is about creating yourself." – George Bernard Shaw

26. "Your time is limited, don't waste it living someone else's life." – Steve Jobs

27. "Living intentionally means making choices that align with your values and beliefs." – Anonymous

28. "You have to decide what your highest priorities are and have the courage—pleasantly, smilingly, non-apologetically—to say 'no' to other things. And the way you do that is by having a bigger 'yes' burning inside." – Stephen Covey

29. "Intentional living is about focusing on what matters most and letting go of the rest." – Anonymous

30. "The only person you are destined to become is the person you decide to be." – Ralph Waldo Emerson

31. "Living intentionally requires us to do something important: slow down." – Anonymous

32. "Intentional living is about making small, deliberate choices every day that add up to a fulfilling life." – Anonymous

33. "If you don't design your own life plan, chances are you'll fall into someone else's plan. And guess what they have planned for you? Not much." – Jim Rohn

34. "When we live intentionally, we become the authors of our own stories." – Anonymous

35. "The best way to predict your future is to create it." – Peter Drucker

36. "Intentional living is not about perfection. It's about making the best choices you can with what you have." – Anonymous

37. "Be intentional with your time. Your future self will thank you." – Anonymous

38. "Intentional living means investing your time and energy in things that truly matter to you." – Anonymous

39. "Living intentionally is about making a difference, not just making a living." – Anonymous

40. "Life is not about finding yourself. It's about creating yourself." – George Bernard Shaw

41. "To live an intentional life, we must first identify what we truly want." – Anonymous

42. "Intentional living is about aligning your actions with your values." – Anonymous

43. "The secret to living intentionally is knowing your 'why.'" – Anonymous

44. "Intentional living is about recognizing that we have the power to shape our own lives." – Anonymous

45. "Living intentionally means prioritizing the things that matter most to you." – Anonymous

46. "Intentional living is the practice of making deliberate choices that lead to a fulfilling life." – Anonymous

47. "Your life becomes much more meaningful when you are intentional about your actions." – Anonymous

48. "Live with purpose. Live with passion. Live intentionally." – Anonymous

49. "Intentional living is about being present and making choices that align with your goals." – Anonymous

50. "To live an intentional life, we must constantly remind ourselves of what is truly important." – Anonymous

Self-Awareness Quotes

1. "The unexamined life is not worth living." – Socrates

2. "To know yourself, you must sacrifice the illusion that you already do." – Vironika Tugaleva

3. "Self-awareness gives you the capacity to learn from your mistakes as well as your successes." – Lawrence Bossidy

4. "Knowing yourself is the beginning of all wisdom." – Aristotle

5. "Without self-awareness, we are as babies in the cradles." – Virginia Woolf

6. "Self-awareness is the key to self-mastery." – Gretchen Rubin

7. "The more self-aware you are, the more self-control you will have." – Anonymous

8. "To become different from what we are, we must have some awareness of what we are." – Eric Hoffer

9. "Your visions will become clear only when you can look into your own heart." – Carl Jung

10. "Self-awareness doesn't stop you from making mistakes, it allows you to learn from them." – Anonymous

11. "He who knows others is wise; he who knows himself is enlightened." – Lao Tzu

12. "Self-awareness allows you to self-correct." – Anonymous

13. "Awareness is the greatest agent for change." – Eckhart Tolle

14. "You cannot change what you are not aware of." – Sheryl Sandberg

15. "Knowing yourself is the beginning of self-love." – Anonymous

16. "Self-awareness is the first step in creating what you want and mastering yourself." – Iyanla Vanzant

17. "The biggest obstacle to self-awareness is self-deception." – Anonymous

18. "Self-awareness brings self-mastery." – Anonymous

19. "Awareness precedes choice and choice precedes results." – Robin Sharma

20. "You can't change what you refuse to confront." – Anonymous

21. "Self-awareness is not just about uncovering your flaws; it's also about recognizing your strengths." – Anonymous

22. "The greatest discovery of any generation is that a human can alter his life by altering his attitude." – William James

23. "Self-awareness is the foundation of personal growth." – Anonymous

24. "The best way to find yourself is to lose yourself in the service of others." – Mahatma Gandhi

25. "Your task is not to seek for love, but merely to seek and find all the barriers within yourself that you have built against it." – Rumi

26. "The more you know yourself, the more clarity there is." – Jiddu Krishnamurti

27. "Self-awareness involves deep personal honesty. It comes from asking and answering hard questions." – Stephen Covey

28. "Without self-awareness, we are as ships without a rudder." – Anonymous

29. "Self-awareness is the ability to take an honest look at your life without any attachment to it being right or wrong." – Debbie Ford

30. "The journey of self-awareness is the most rewarding journey of all." – Anonymous

31. "When I discover who I am, I'll be free." – Ralph Ellison

32. "Self-awareness is the key to unlocking your true potential." – Anonymous

33. "Self-awareness is the ability to step outside yourself and see yourself with the eyes of others." – Anonymous

34. "A man who knows himself can step outside himself and watch his own reactions like an observer." – Adam Smith

35. "Self-awareness is the capacity to stand apart from ourselves and examine our thinking, our motives, our history, our actions, and our habits and tendencies." – Stephen Covey

36. "Self-awareness is not the same as self-approval, any more than imagination is the same as day-dreaming." – Francis Spufford

37. "Self-awareness is the key to a conscious life." – Anonymous

38. "In a world that constantly tries to shape you into something else, self-awareness is your greatest weapon." – Anonymous

39. "Be mindful. Be grateful. Be positive. Be true. Be kind." – Roy T. Bennett

40. "To know yourself, you must first sacrifice the illusion that you already do." – Vironika Tugaleva

41. "With self-awareness, we know how to respond to situations mindfully instead of reacting mindlessly." – Anonymous

42. "Self-awareness is the foundation for meaningful change." – Anonymous

43. "The most fundamental form of human stupidity is forgetting what we were trying to do in the first place." – Friedrich Nietzsche

44. "True self-awareness is the courage to be yourself, even when it is unpopular." – Anonymous

45. "The better you know yourself, the better your relationship with the rest of the world." – Toni Collette

46. "The more you understand yourself, the more patience you have for what you see in others." – Erik Erikson

47. "Self-awareness is the greatest asset anyone can possess." – Anonymous

48. "A wise man is not taught by his own words but by the words of others." – Anonymous

49. "Self-awareness enables you to align your actions with your values." – Anonymous

50. "To know oneself is to study oneself in action with another person." – Bruce Lee

Conclusion

Congratulations. You've made it to the end of *Living to Impress Sucks: The Dangers of a Faked Life and How to Let Go of Your Constant Need for Approval.* I will end it all by reminding you of the key points and insights you've been learning. For a goodbye, I will leave you with additional actions steps and resources to advance your dream of an improved life lived on your own terms.

Summary of Key Points

1. Understanding the Habit of Impressing Others: We talked about the psychological and societal factors that drive the need to impress others, including the role of early influences, media, and peer pressure.

2. Recognizing Your False Identity: We identified techniques for self-reflection and self-awareness. They will help you identify patterns of behaviour aimed at impressing others so you can begin to rediscover and reconnect with your true self.

3. Breaking Free from the Habit: In one section, we saw the practical steps needed to build authenticity, set boundaries, and develop healthy relationships. These steps included intentional living, accepting your true self, practising self-compassion, and focusing on meaningful connections.

4. Discovering Intentional Living

Further, we uncovered the hidden truths in finding peace and contentment through intentional living. A simplified life can be an antidote to the constant need to seek external validation.

5. Sustaining Change: Finally, we learnt key strategies for creating lasting habits. Areas emphasized include the importance of consistency, patience, and alignment with your core values and passions. You also got access to inspirational quotes about trying to impress others to help you stay motivated and energized on your chosen path to a more authentic and fulfilling lifestyle.

My Last Words of Encouragement to You

You will have by now realized that the road to setting yourself free from a constant need for external validation is both challenging and rewarding. It's a path of self-discovery, growth, and transformation that requires courage and perseverance. Here are some final words of encouragement as you continue on this journey.

Be Patient with Yourself: Personal growth is a gradual process. Be patient and compassionate with yourself as you navigate the ups and downs. Celebrate your progress, no matter how small, and learn from setbacks without harsh self-judgment.

Understand You Cannot Be Perfect: Authenticity doesn't mean being perfect. So let your imperfections and vulnerabilities be a source of strength and inspiration rather than a barrier to a better life. Always remember that they are part of what makes you unique and genuine. And don't forget, it's okay to make mistakes and learn from them.

Remain True to Your Values: Let your core values guide your decisions and actions. When you live in alignment with your personal values, you create a life that is meaningful and fulfilling. Trust yourself and stay committed to what matters most to you.

Seek Support: Do not hesitate to ask others you trust for help. Surround yourself with supportive and like-minded individuals who encourage your growth and admire your quest for a life that reflects who you truly are. Seek out communities, online platforms, mentors, life coaches and friends who are willing to support, inspire and uplift you.

Reflect and Learn While You Grow: Personal growth is an ongoing journey. Continue to reflect on your experiences, seek new insights, and remain open to change and new ideas. As you grow, your understanding of your true self and purpose may evolve. The most exciting part is that it will lead you to new opportunities for a truly fulfilling life.

A Call to Action

Now that you've understood the dangers of living to impress others and learned practical ways to embrace authenticity, it's time to take action.

Start implementing the insights and strategies you've gained from this book into your daily life.

Take small, consistent steps towards living a life that reflects your true self and values.

Remember, the journey to authenticity is a personal and unique path - pursue it with an open heart and a courageous spirit.

Additional Resources for Further Reading and Practice

See below some recommended resources for further reading, reinforcement and support. By utilizing these resources, you can continue to deepen your understanding and practice of authenticity, leading to a more fulfilling and meaningful life.

1. Books

The Gifts of Imperfection by Brené Brown

Daring Greatly by Brené Brown

Radical Acceptance by Tara Brach

The Power of Now by Eckhart Tolle

Atomic Habits by James Clear

The Life-Changing Magic of Tidying Up by Marie Kondo

The Art of Happiness by Dalai Lama and Howard Cutler

2. Online Courses and Workshops

Personal growth and self-improvement courses on platforms like Coursera, Udemy, MasterClass and Skillshare

Coursera (coursera.org)

- *The Science of Well-Being*

Offered by: Yale University

Description: This course explores what psychological science says about living a happy and fulfilling life

Cost: Free to audit, with a fee for a certificate.

- *Introduction to Personal Branding*

Offered by: University of Virginia

Description: Learn how to create a strong personal brand.

Cost: Free to audit, with a fee for a certificate.

- *Financial Planning for Young Adults*

Offered by: University of Illinois at Urbana-Champaign

Description: Learn about managing personal finances, budgeting, and investing, essential for achieving financial freedom.

Cost: Free to audit, with a fee for a certificate.

- Mindshift: Break Through Obstacles to Learning and Discover Your Hidden Potential

Offered by: McMaster University

Description: This course helps you overcome learning obstacles and discover new ways to develop your potential.

Cost: Free to audit, with a fee for a certificate.

- Learning How to Learn: Powerful mental tools to help you master tough subjects

Offered by: McMaster University, University of California San Diego

Description: This course provides practical techniques to help you learn more effectively, a valuable skill for lifelong learning.

Cost: Free to audit, with a fee for a certificate.

Mindfulness-Based Stress Reduction (MBSR) programs

Insight Timer (insighttimer.com)

Udemy (udemy.com)

Workshops, videos and webinars by renowned self-help authors and speakers

Brian Tracy

John C. Maxwell

Gary Thomas

Tony Robbins

Self-Improvement YouTube Channels

3. Support Groups and Communities

Online forums and communities focused on personal growth and authenticity.

Local support groups and meetups for individuals seeking to live more authentically

4. Websites and Blogs

Zen Habits (zenhabits.net)

Becoming Minimalist (becomingminimalist.com)

Mindful (mindful.org)

Tiny Buddha (tinybuddha.com)

The Minimalists (theminimalists.com)

5. Professional Help

Therapy and counselling services for personalized support and guidance

Life coaching to help you achieve your goals and maintain your progress

6. Exercises and Worksheets

Values Exploration Worksheet*

- List your top 10 values.

- Reflect on how each value influences your decisions and actions.

- Identify areas where your actions may not align with your values and set goals to address them.

Gratitude Journal Prompts

- List three things you are grateful for today.

- Reflect on a challenging situation and identify something positive you learned from it.

- Write about a person you appreciate and why they are important to you.

Mindfulness Practices

- Morning meditation: Spend 5-10 minutes focusing on your breath and setting an intention for the day.

- Mindful eating: Pay full attention to the taste, texture, and aroma of your food during a meal.

- Body scan meditation: Spend 10-15 minutes focusing on sensations in different parts of your body, from head to toe.

Goal-Setting Worksheet

- Identify one short-term and one long-term goal that aligns with your values.

- Use the SMART criteria to define each goal.

- Break down the goals into actionable steps and set deadlines for each step.

Decluttering Checklist

- List areas of your home or workspace that need decluttering.

- Prioritize the areas and set a schedule for tackling each one.

- For each area, sort items into categories: keep, donate, sell, discard.

7. References

1. Tolle, E. (1997). *The Power of Now*. Namaste Publishing.

2. Clear, J. (2018). *Atomic Habits: An Easy & Proven Way to Build Good Habits & Break Bad Ones. Avery.*

3. Kondo, M. (2014). *The Life-Changing Magic of Tidying Up: The Japanese Art of Decluttering and Organizing.* Ten Speed Press.

4. Dalai Lama, & Cutler, H. (1998). *The Art of Happiness*: A Handbook for Living. Riverhead Books.

5. Brown, B. (2012). *Daring Greatly: How the Courage to Be Vulnerable Transforms the Way We Live, Love, Parent, and Lead.* Gotham Books.

Thank you for choosing the path towards a more authentic life anchored on intentional living. Remember, every small step you take brings you closer to a life of authenticity, fulfilment, and happiness.

Implement the process and stay committed to your values. This way, you will never regret the decision to join many others who are already on this odyssey to self-discovery and growth.

TIME FOR ACTION

Unlock the power of personal growth with our expert-guided courses. Start your journey to a better you today!

THE END

Don't miss out!

Visit the website below and you can sign up to receive emails whenever Ralph Nyadzi publishes a new book. There's no charge and no obligation.

https://books2read.com/r/B-A-OQZF-HTVUD

BOOKS 2 READ

Connecting independent readers to independent writers.

Did you love *Living to Impress Sucks*? Then you should read *What Makes A Hater*[1] by Ralph Nyadzi!

[2]

In a world where success often breeds jealousy and ambition can spark envy and bare-faced hatred, understanding and overcoming these toxic emotions is crucial for personal and professional growth. What Makes a Hater delves deep into the roots of jealousy, envy and hatred. It uncovers why you attract these negative sentiments and provides practical strategies to rise above them.

Drawing on psychological insights, real-life case studies, and proven self-improvement techniques, this book offers a comprehensive guide to recognizing the signs of envy in yourself and others. Learn how to set healthy boundaries, build emotional resilience, and transform negativity into motivation. From managing professional

---

1. https://books2read.com/u/4AXOKN

2. https://books2read.com/u/4AXOKN

jealousy in the workplace to nurturing positive personal relationships, "What Makes a Hater" equips you with the tools to navigate a world rife with envy and emerge stronger, more confident, and ultimately, more successful.

The contents of this book will inspire you to act with courage and build a life that moves beyond jealousy and hatred. You will discover how to turn the challenges posed by envy into opportunities for growth and fulfilment. Whether you're looking to improve your career, strengthen your relationships, or enhance your overall well-being, this book is your roadmap to thriving amidst negativity and realizing your dream of lasting happiness.

Read more at https://www.cegastacademy.com.

Also by Ralph Nyadzi

Fast Track WASSCE General Arts
Fast Track WASSCE Government: Elements of Government

Standalone
Regrets
The Self-Support Guide
Becoming Self-Employed
Understanding Grammatical Names and Functions
Second Class Citizen Summary & Analysis
The Lion and the Jewel Summary & Analysis
WAEC Literature Poetry: Summary & Analysis
WAEC Literature African Poetry Summary & Analysis
WAEC Literature Non-African Poetry Summary & Analysis
What Makes A Hater
Living to Impress Sucks

Watch for more at https://www.cegastacademy.com.

About the Author

Ralph Nyadzi is the founder of **RN Diggital** - a digital publishing and content marketing agency for small local businesses. He teaches English for Academic Purposes (EAP) online and blogs at Cegast Academy and BloggingtotheMax.com. Besides writing full-time, he enjoys cooking and farming. Ralph lives in the coastal belt of Ghana, his native country.

Read more at https://www.cegastacademy.com.

About the Publisher

Cegast Academy is the sole publisher of books authored by Ralph Nyadzi and other authors who are happy to work with him.

Read more at https://www.cegastacademy.com/.